Wake Up Dead Man

A Quick Brown Fox Publications Book

First published in Great Britain by Quick Brown Fox Publications in 2007; this edition published by Quick Brown Fox Publications in 2007

Copyright © Matt Stephens 2007.
Edited by Adam Kirkman.
Produced in partnership with Global.

The moral right of the author has been asserted.
All characters in this publication other than those clearly in the public domain are fictitious and any resemblance to real persons, living or dead, is purely coincidental.

All rights reserved. No part of this publication may be reproduced, stored in a retrieval system, or transmitted in any form or by any means, without the prior permission in writing of the publisher, nor be otherwise circulated in any form of binding or cover other than that in which it is published and without a similar condition including this condition being imposed on the subsequent purchaser.

ISBN-10 0955480426   ISBN-13 9780955480423

Cover image © Michael Sullivan, 2007. Used with permission.
Cover design by Paul Martin.

Quick Brown Fox Publications is an independent literary agency and publishers. They want to hear from first time authors so please get in touch. They'd love to hear from you. Contact them at feedback@quickbrownfoxpublications.co.uk. Please recommend this book to a friend as they'd be very grateful.
www.quickbrownfoxpublications.co.uk

www.globalyork.com

www.wakeupdeadman.co.uk

Wake Up Dead Man

Matt Stephens

Published by Quick Brown Fox Publications, 2007

*"Jesus, Jesus help me,
I'm alone in this world,
And a f***** up world it is too,
Tell me, tell me the story,
The one about eternity,
And the way it's all gonna be...
Wake up, wake up dead man,
Wake up, wake up dead man..."*
Bono, *Pop*, 1997.

Amanda, I love you.
Noah, you're the man.
Global, you're awesome.
God, I hope it achieves what we talked about!

The Church Is Dying.

There comes a moment when you realise there's no point continuing. The body is biologically dead and the spirit has departed, the ship has sunk, the war is lost, the game is over and the whistle has been blown. Many people are saying something similar about the church in the West today. It's done and dusted, past its sell-by date and, in many ways, they are right.

The church seems to be in terminal decline, its heyday well and truly gone. Attendance is at an all time low, church buildings are being sold off to become pubs or clubs, the authority of its leaders is being questioned, secularism is rampant, Islam is on the rise, visions and dreams are dying and church morality is as low as that in society - understand the picture, THINGS ARE NOT GOOD.

So is this another book simply lamenting the state of the church in the West, and in particular, Britain?
NO.
This book is about two things:

1. To have a no holds barred look at the current reality of the Church today, to raise our awareness of how bad the situation really is so that we shift the debate from 'should we or shouldn't we change' to 'if we don't change NOW we are sunk!'

2. To offer some practical steps to get us from the current reality to a future fulfilling the vision of what the church can and should be like according to its founding members. One of the most vital steps will be to lay out the reason for the need to re-introduce an **abundance mindset** back into the church.

However, BEWARE - these steps are not easy, they will cost and they will mean losing friends, gaining enemies and moving on, and that's just *within* the church!

My message is far from one of love and peace at the cost of all else - my message is more like Jesus' message when He said:

> *Do not suppose that I have come to bring peace to the earth. I did not come to bring peace, but a sword. For I have come to turn a man against his father, a daughter against her mother, a daughter-in-law against her mother-in-law - a man's enemies will be the members of his own household.*
> (*Matthew 10 v34-6, NIV*)

My hope is that this book will inspire and start a revolution - for the time is well and truly gone for an evolution. We need the Church of England, Baptists, Methodists, the Free Church, Pentecostals, the lot - to **WAKE UP** and let the REVOLUTION begin, let the adrenaline surge as the gloves come off and the fight for the local church begins.

First, Get Mad!

Imagine with me for a moment...

The devil sitting on his mock throne, surveying the situation he's so • **scared** as he looks across the world at the local churches • **scared** of the political correctness • **scared** of the wackiness • **scared** of the bureaucracy • **scared** of the slowness • **scared** of the same sixty people turning out for church, faithfully growing old together and enjoying it being a private club just for them • **scared** of the people falling over in the spirit while at yet another revival meeting • **scared** of the yearly united evangelistic week in the city which ticks all the boxes but sees very few saved • **scared** of the all the introspection and the 'what about me' brigade • **scared** of the people asleep during worship • **scared** of the faithless people who believe in poverty and that miracles were for biblical times only • **scared** of the just-for-Sunday crew • **scared** of the 'talk the talk' but never 'walk the walk' crew • **scared** of strawberries and Pimms at the pastor's house • **scared** of the vicar preaching about whether the government is right or wrong • **scared** of the coffee mornings • **scared** of the weekly small group that people religiously turn up to • **scared** of the disregarded buildings • **scared** of the faithful few who turn to out to pray each week with no expectation of change • **scared** of the leaders who won't even stand up to their own congregation.

Can you imagine letting the sheep lead the shepherd? You don't have to, it's rife in the church.

• **scared** of the fear • **scared** of the 'let's take a year out and travel the world' gang • **scared** of the 'I need a break' group who believe church is too demanding - read the Bible, Jesus promised blood, sweat and toil and for it - reward in this life and the next! • **scared** of the summer camps (what have they achieved, apart from reminding thousands of young people how they don't have a church that will keep up their passion! Now, if we renamed them 'how to become a change insurgent for God' or 'let's change the world NOW' camps which didn't just last the summer, maybe we'd be onto something.)

Oh yes, he's • **scared** of the Christian Unions on campuses all over the country - now this one I could talk about forever, CUs have become the single biggest barrier to their own vision of affecting Universities for God. Just ask any non-Christian and they'll tell you that the CU are a bunch of saddos, or they've never heard of it, or that it's full of freaks and you know what, sometimes they're not wrong! Why? So much politics, so many people thinking they can make a difference but without the guidance and long term plan it needs: it's delusion at its most grand, and its most destructive.

But let me tell you what I see for Universities, I see an army of young people who are leaderless and I am desperate for them to be led into war.

They are armed to the teeth with weaponry, but don't use it. Instead, they meet together in little groups and 'hang out', debating whether there should be hand raising in CU or whether they should pray in tongues. It's a waste and it's criminal.

Hopefully, you've picked up my sarcasm. Trouble is, the devil's not scared. He's loving it.

Let's take a second here.

Get it.

Let what I have said sink in, I want you to feel my total and utter anger and pain, feel the passion and love, and let it get you angry. Let it get you good and mad because then you just might act.

We won't change until the pain becomes too much, change only happens when we are no longer willing to live with the situation - usually because it's too painful: think about losing weight, leaving a partner, changing jobs...

We often make the change when the pain in our world drives us to taking the action required. Right now as you survey the situation there is not enough pain and anger, frustration and rage at the state of the church. You hear comments like "it's not that bad" or "there's no need to get so worked up." Yet every single indicator possible tells us that for the last however long the church has been in terminal decline. In any other business, in any other sector, all the red flags would have gone up a long time ago - but not the church!

Get the point.
We need to

GET MAD!

Now, Imagine This...

I can see a church rising up that is full of righteous anger, excitement, determination, passion and resilience, a church that is beginning to take action, that is fearless, and I can imagine the devil looking out on a totally different scene...

There is • **fear** as he sees leaders who are strong with great vision and a flexible 'let's give it a go' attitude - think Paul Scanlon, think Archbishop Sentamu, think Colin Dye, think Terry Virgo - these are some, but we need more. And if you don't know those names, it's definitely time that you did.

He's • **in fear** of a relevant, credible church that is aware of and thinks about non-Christians • **in fear** of a fast-thinking, lean church that can adapt in a heartbeat • **in fear** of a growing church that's attracting new people to come and hear the awesome message we have been given.

His • **fear** of a church where over half of the congregation are under thirty years old • **fear** of a church full of kids and young people who passionately worship and sing the songs at school and on the street because they're as cool as what's in the charts.

There's • **fear** of a church that is so naturally supernatural, just like the early church in Acts 2 where the supernatural benefits secular society, oh yes, he's • **in fear** of a church that IS evangelism rather than tries to DO evangelism - it's a way of life, not an activity or an afterthought!

He's quaking with • **fear** of a church that exists for those who don't belong to it - now how old is that one! • **Fearful** of a church where the very presence of God can be felt during worship, where people are healed, strengthened and led to Christ.

Imagine his • **fear** as he sees a church full of people who understand and who love doing church 24/7, forgetting balance and instead give all to Christ every day, whether at work or at night on the streets doing youth work, or any number of activities that will benefit the communities they live in.

There's • **fear** as he looks out and sees a church where the people love to be with those who don't know God, reaching them with the good news of Jesus. Now this may be through going for a beer with them and listening to them, or babysitting, or meeting other needs.

• **fear** as he sees a church where the pastor is unpredictable and challenging and is more likely to have a curry night where the local chavs turn up than host a Pimms and strawberries snooze-fest.

Can you imagine his • **fear** as he hears reports that preaching on Sundays makes an impact and is thought-provoking and challenging? Where everyone is getting the principles of God and being able to apply them to their lives? His • **fear** as he sees state of the art venues being built all over the country in towns, cities and villages, venues that rival anything that the world is doing and becoming a magnet for people who are devoted to doing and being church as a lifestyle?

You can almost smell the • **fear** as he sees a church that is taught to pray continually and while on the move, rather than once a week at the 'pity party' prayer meeting, oh yes, taste his • **fear** as young people have an option other than University or minimum wage slave labour - the option to stay at their local church and play a major role in taking the kingdom into their city.

His • **fear** when all those who hold 'pity parties' and who so often claimed that they 'need a break' begin to rise up, believing the promises of God, being healed to become the walking wounded who won't stop but fight on, using their experiences to make them stronger, more determined and more desperate for breakthrough for God and His Kingdom!

Imagine his • **fear** seeing young people going to University and getting plugged into their local church so that they then reach into the University in relevant and credible ways - where the debates they have are how to reach more people faster, further and more effectively, where they put on the best bar crawls in town and there isn't anyone vomiting into a urine-stained nightclub toilet at the end!

And let's not forget the summer camps, as I'm sure he'll try to, as they move into the cities not occasionally but every year as churches (working together or alone - who really cares, as long as they're *working*) putting on weekly kids clubs and youth groups and evangelistic events and street cleaning and and and...not one summer but every summer, every year, everywhere!

We don't have to imagine this, we can make it a reality!

So let the **REVOLUTION** begin!

Yes, it will be **MESSY** but just look at the book of Acts or in fact any of the Apostle Paul's letters - pioneering work is, always has been, and always will be

MESSY!

Part 1: Time To Face The Truth

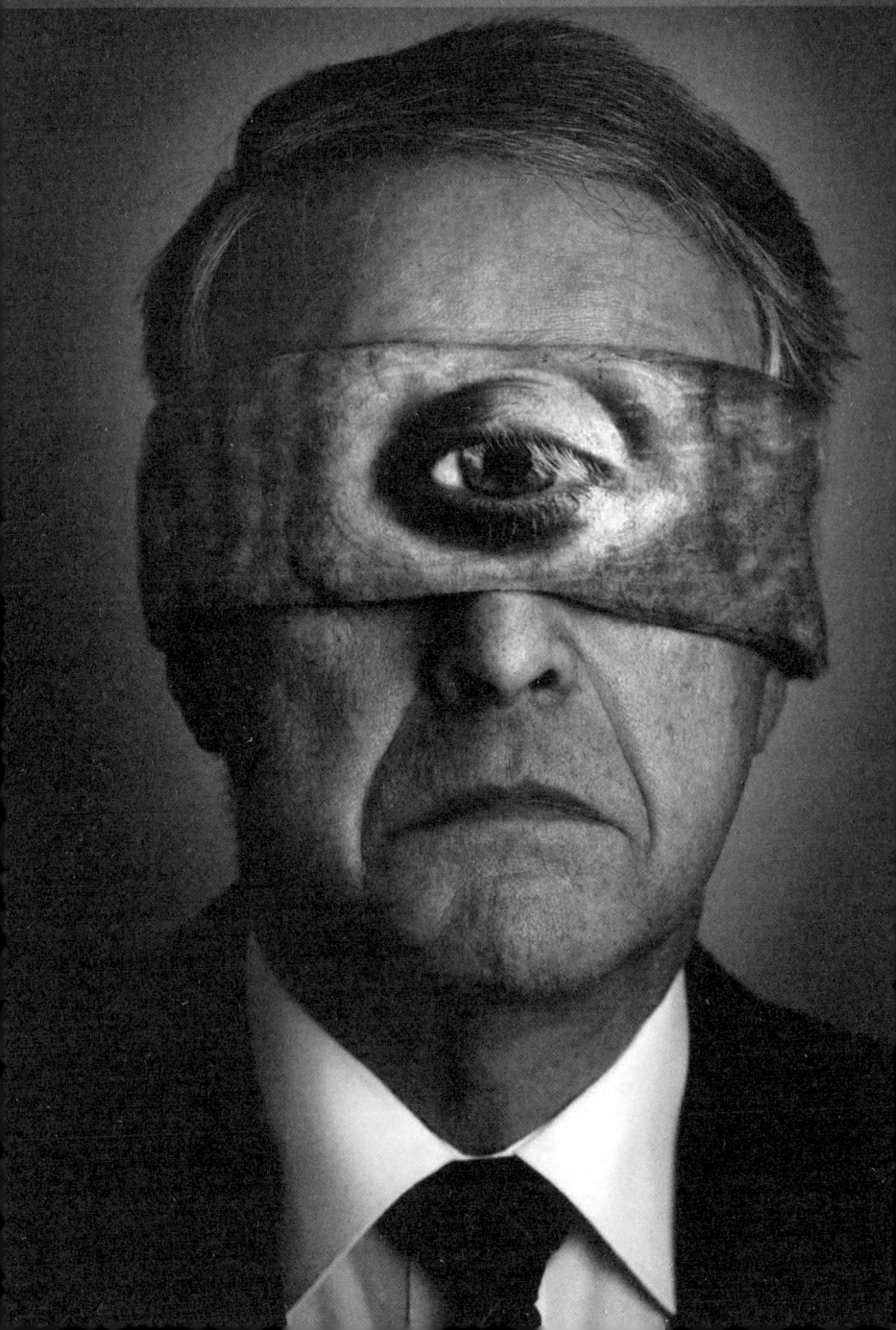

The local church is the hope of the world.

Bill Hybels said that the local church is the hope of the world, and I agree. In fact, I believe it so much that I have given my life to take God's strategic choice and to pour everything I have into the local church.

Think what we could do with twelve dedicated people. Think how much we could achieve and what could be sparked into life, affecting towns, cities and ultimately nations if people gave all they had - time, money, energy, skills, abilities - to the local church.

It's happened before, two thousand years ago, and we need it to happen again. But where are our twelve?

So now it's time to be truthful, to look at the situation as it really is - and I'm asking, is anyone out there seeing what I am seeing? The church is in **Massive Decline**. We seek shelter in the fantasy that more prayer will solve it, or even that God himself will somehow intervene and turn the situation around - but remember the stories in the Old Testament?

Israel carried off into **captivity**, Jerusalem **destroyed**, the Temple **gone**?

If we don't **wake up** and smell the coffee, read the signs of the times like Jesus told us to do, then we will **sleep walk** into **oblivion**:

He said to the crowd: 'When you see a cloud rising in the west, immediately you say, 'It's going to rain,' and it does. And when the south wind blows, you say, 'It's going to be hot,' and it is. Hypocrites! You know how to interpret the appearance of the earth and the sky. How is it that you don't know how to interpret this present time?'
(*Luke 12 v54-56, NIV*)

Tell me you're not ignoring it, but that it makes you as **angry** as me.

Worse news still: it's our own fault.

RANDOM QUESTION

? *Why would leaders listen to the same forty people who got the church into a mess to help get them out of it?*

Please ponder the above and let it sink in. **By all means, get angry.** Get something. Reconnect to your emotions, so that they drive you to seek a solution, to seek change. Let the pain of it cause you to look for change. **Pain is one of the greatest motivating forces in the universe as it causes us to change.**

Please don't be another person who ignores this, who turns away, closes their ears and carries on as if it will all work out anyway!

Remember that when the *Titanic* launched in 1911, it was heralded as something amazing, something incredible, that it was the future. As we've all seen from the Leonardo DiCaprio and Kate Winslet film, everything was great on board initially: but when disaster struck, things changed.

But did the **attitude** of those on board?

There were still those who kept the commoners locked below while the ship was sinking. There was a captain who led recklessly. There were lifeboats launched half empty; there were riots; there were musicians playing on hopelessly.

Any of this familiar?

TIME TO FACE THE TRUTH:
THE *TITANIC* SANK!

At no point did anyone face facts that the ship was sinking and they were going to die.

It's the same with the church.

TIME FOR SOME SHOCKING FACTS -

Between 1998 and 2005, **half a million** people stopped going to church on Sunday.

The Daily Telegraph's religious affairs correspondent Jonathan Petre says, "While a thousand new people are joining a church each week, **two and a half thousand are leaving.**"

Only **6.3%** of the population go to church on an average Sunday, compared to **7.5%** in 1998.

Almost a third of churchgoers are aged 65 or over, compared to the 16% it was in 1998.

Sunday churchgoing is **declining** at **2.3%** a year.

Nearly all church growth is **false growth**, due to immigrants: due to new EU regulations, a massive influx of Polish workers have filled some churches.

The **drop** in attendance in the 20-29 age group was **29%**.

National Attendance

1979	👥👥👥👥👥👥	12%
1989	👥👥👥👥👥	10%
1998	👥👥👥👥	7.5%
2005	👥👥👥	6.3%
2015	3.0%??	
2025	0.0%??	

In April 2007, Tearfund's report on churchgoing in the UK found that:

26 million adults claim to be Christian and of that 26 million, only 7.6 million adults go to church each month.
- 12.6 million people go at least once a year.
- 32 million people have no connection with church.
- 3 million people would go to church *if asked*.

How shocking is that?!

(Maybe we should ask them...)

Take this on board: the church is

sinking.

It's worse than the *Titanic*, as that was only a ship: the church's death has **eternal consequences**.

Listen up:

"The Church of England is between a rock and a hard place, and there are bitter pills to be swallowed. The most painful fact with which it has to deal (along with other churches) is the all-round drop in numbers: churchgoers, those on the electoral roles, numbers of baptisms, confirmations, church weddings - all have dropped steadily since the 1930s, with consequential loss both of morals and of income.

"Much is made of the increase in the numbers of ordinands (those training for the priesthood), but this, the only good news on the table at the time of writing, seems an odd criterion of renewed life - many chiefs and few Indians will scarcely solve the problem.

"Children who do not come from churchgoing homes - as I did not - now grow up largely ignorant of Christian ideas in a way unimaginable half a century ago...The comments about religion by journalists in the press and on television...suggest that even the basic Christian ideas are no longer understood by university-educated people, still

less by others. Indeed even churchgoers can reveal an ignorance of the main elements of Christian belief."
    (Monica Furlong, *Church of England: The State It's In*)

One single trend emerges from all the statistics of religious belief in the UK: our population is predominantly irreligious, profoundly innocent and ignorant of religion, despite some defaulting to calling themselves 'Christian.' (71%)

The country is not Christian, despite a vague and half-hearted belief in a God of some sort.

The prophet Ezekiel, writing five thousand years ago, had a funny message, which went something like this - he saw a nation that was falling apart:

THERE WAS NO RESPECT FOR GOD'S WAYS.

ITS CRIME RATE WAS SOARING.

SEXUAL DEVIANCY WAS ON THE RISE.

MISUSE OF POWER WAS COMMONPLACE.

SOCIAL EXPLOITATION WAS RAMPANT.

ITS LEADERSHIP HAD FAILED.

Sound familiar?

The political hierarchy has ignored God's principles for life. This is nothing new, it's happened repeatedly throughout history, but when it's joined by the loss of a **relevant** and **credible** church - it means all hopes for society are lost.

Our church is riddled with 'does my bum look big in this?' leadership. Popularity is too important to our church leaders. They ask the question,

'Do you agree with God?'

And then meekly add, 'If not...we will change.'

It's time we learn that the church is an army, sure it's got a hospital wing, but that's to patch you up and put you back into the fight, not to keep you hooked up on a machine, draining resources from the time you're eight to the time you're eighty.

Doing the same thing over and over again and expecting a different outcome is a sure sign of **madness**. If you drop a pen a hundred times from a table, do you expect anything different than for it to hit the floor a hundred times?

Would a wall be any less solid if you tried to run through it once a week for ten years than if you tried it once, and then gave up and used the door?

Churches that do the **same thing** and look for a **different outcome** show signs of **madness** - on an institutional level.

We can't keep doing what we have been doing and expect a different result. We need a whole new way of being and doing - which starts with thinking in a different way.

Just look at Jesus. He was a new solution for a new time - part of a long-term plan, yes, but He recognised change, He adapted and He innovated - look at His empowerment of women, His embracing of the poor, the new covenant, and above all, the arrival and blessing of grace and favour!

What is so frustrating for Ezekiel, and for me, and I hope for you too, is that God is struggling to find anyone from within the church who will **stand up** and **shout** at the **top of their lungs...**

'IN GOD'S NAME AND FOR GOD'S SAKE, STOP! WE ARE DYING, THE NATION IS FAILING AND WE ARE TO BLAME! *WE NEED TO CHANGE*.'

But, irony of ironies, we blame the world! That is so bittersweet when we have always been told in the Bible that the world will always be the world and we should expect no less from them, but to be **sold out by the church verges on sickening.**

The point I'm trying to make (and maybe not very well) is that the situation isn't great, in fact, it's a lot worse than that. We need to get our heads out of the sand and acknowledge it is **time** to **do** something **different**.

What follows next is my experience, and it shows us the state of the church today. How I wish this wasn't my story, but I hope it will make you laugh, I hope it makes you cry, but most of all, I hope it will **connect** with you - perhaps uncomfortably.

Good.

Story Time!

So another service came to an end and once again we all streamed out into the foyer of the secondary school where we met as a church. Why were we tucked away in a school on a Sunday? We were all desperate to get past Henry Hugger and George Groper, two men who were given the title 'ushers' but would be more accurately described as 'desperate men in need of attention.' This is always something that had fascinated me, how on earth the usher team could be made up of dodgy, cardigan wearing, big Bible carrying men - and even scarier looking women who looked as if they were going to cry if you spoke to them!

As I made my way out into the foyer I was confronted with the classic dilemma of how to avoid being asked to lunch by one of what became termed the 'usual suspects.' Now, there's nothing wrong with being invited for lunch, but I had made the mistake once of saying yes to the invite (early on in my church life - I was young and naïve, what can I say? Like most students, I was bowled over by the thought of a free roast.) Well, since that first (and yes, only) dinner, I had studiously avoided being asked again, always careful to avoid the 'usual suspects' and when, on the (rare) occasion they had got to me, I had perfected feigning other commitments. Comments like, 'I'd really love to but...' or 'that is so kind, but sadly I have to...' I had a long list prepared well in advance of things I would say I had to do. None of them important, of course, but all of them better than that few hours with 'good church folk.'

What I really wanted to say was 'thank you, but there is no way I would come and spend three hours listening to why the drums are too loud,' or about 'how we used to really get filled with the Spirit,' or make polite conversation with someone who I have absolutely nothing in common with, except that we attend the same church service each week.

But I never did say those things, at least, not out loud, they weren't allowed because that was being honest and in our church that really was the most mortal of sins.

Anyway, I was now in line for my free cold coffee and stale biscuit, I never wanted them, never really knew why I always queued in the foyer of this secondary school, waiting to be taken back home. Somehow, queuing felt better than standing around gormlessly, waiting to be pounced on by someone who (with all the enthusiasm they could muster) would say 'Hey hey, have you ever thought about joining the kids work? Or becoming part of the usher team? Or coming along early to help set up?' All appealing options, really.

After politely declining, making sure to make clear that the one thing God had definitely told me was that I was specifically not called for any and all of those things (always a winner, as they can't argue with something God told you directly) they would suddenly lose all their enthusiasm, saying something like, 'I don't blame you really, it's so much hard work and there's so few of us, I only joined because someone made me,' it pretty much put me off ever wanting to 'get involved,' with all its insidious consequences.

So, I finally collected my free coffee from the table and moved further into the foyer. I could see Derek, our pastor, being clobbered again by the same few people who always made sure they told him what they had thought of the service. Today they seemed particularly animate, waving their hands in the air and making lots of crazy facial expressions. By now, I knew that this meant that they were pleased and felt he had 'hit the mark.' (Phew. I was glad that Derek could sleep tonight with their approval sewn up for another week.)

When they didn't approve, they would have more of a finger jabbing approach, with serious and stern faces. This was another ritual of our church, that the same few people would give feedback to our pastor so he was sure how they thought it had gone and whether any correction or change of direction was needed. Someone had once dubbed them the 'rabble' and that had stuck ever since. (I found out later that was to do with the rabble in the desert who made Moses' life so difficult when leading the people of Israel into the Promised Land.)

In an attempt to not come across as an arrogant or shepherding leader, or appear offensive, or in fact, come across as *anything* at all, Derek had to 'humble' himself to prove he was a real leader - naturally, a real leader being someone who was led by the people. Although I had heard on the grapevine (not gossip, of course, that's never to be found in the church) that he had confronted the rabble once only to have found himself in a worse situation.

He invited the rabble leaders round to talk about the future of the church and the need for co-operation and for people to follow - and what did follow was that, straight after the meeting, two of the rabble said they had been mortally wounded by what Derek had said and had sought counselling to help them through the vicious and unfounded attack. I tell you now with the benefit of hindsight and forgiveness, it really would be funny if it wasn't so darn serious.

Of course, like me you're wondering, 'what did Derek say?' He told them he needed their co-operation, and that if they didn't like the direction he was taking and how he was leading then there were other good churches they could attend in the area, because who would want to stay at a church where they complained more than they were happy?

Needless to say, the rabble didn't want to leave and (worse!) denied ever stirring up or causing ill-feeling, and made a big deal about how they now needed counselling to help them through the lack of love shown by their pastor. Again, it would be funny if it wasn't so true.

The upshot was the pastor ended up holding more meetings with them at which he was urged to apologise to prove his love and help rehabilitate them back into church life. The reality was that they never stopped attending - only for that period they were so 'hurt', which was soon 'healed' with lots of love and attention.

However, today had been reasonable, the rabble had approved, and as I sipped my cold coffee (was there ever any sugar?) I realised that even I had managed to take something from the talk about King David. I'll be honest, I had always liked David: he seemed to have a sense of adventure about him and wasn't afraid to get things wrong. I also liked the fact that he seemed to be really passionate about God - a characteristic that I seemed to have lost, and couldn't be further away from this school foyer.

I had always identified with David, thinking that when I grew up, I would be just like him: strong, courageous and passionate for God. I wondered where it had all gone wrong, how had I ended up so cynical and critical.

I mean, I hadn't always been like this, only four years ago I had been at a summer camp, one of the large ones they hold each year in a field somewhere in the south of England. It was amazing, I had come across thousands of young people passionate and on fire for God, we had sung and sung with the worship time lasting what seemed like moments but had actually been hours. We had dedicated ourselves to God, sitting up late in the large tent that I shared with nine other lads, praying for each other, dreaming about how we were going to change this nation, see God do miracles and marry beautiful Christian women. We had seen the future and it looked so bright.

Now here I was, completely disillusioned just two years into adult church life and the passion had been drained away within the first six months just like the heat from my coffee. I had joined this church as it was meant to be a 'good one' and at first it was – it seemed to have all the hallmarks of a passionate church, although not *too* passionate.

Although isn't it funny how in worship EVERYONE seems to be looking at you? I call it the spotlight effect. In fact, I think the first time I raised my hands in worship, later referred to as the Hand Raising Incident, I felt like everyone was looking at me, although they were probably looking at the rather pretty student sat to my right.

But it was hard to be passionate when, after scratching the surface, you realised most of the lifers (people who had managed to attend for over ten years) seemed to have issues and when I had been cornered into going for lunch they talked about the passion they used to have, how in the good old days they had got up early for prayer meetings, had all night worship times, walked the streets singing in tongues and saw angels riverdancing on their duvets but now they only talked about coming to church out of duty as if that was a suitable replacement for passion.

"Matt, good to see you - did you enjoy the service today?"
For once, I didn't have to lie. "Yes, thanks, it was good - especially Derek's talk on David."
"Great, great. Now, what I was wondering was whether you were coming to the prayer meeting this evening?"
Ah, the weekly prayer meeting. A whole kettle of vitriol in itself. I had a flashback to the last time I went, only six weeks since I had fallen for that question previously.
Jasper was our prayer co-ordinator (why he needed the title, I wasn't sure, and what he did in terms of co-ordinating prayer was even more unclear) and he had asked me if I would like to come along to the prayer meeting. I knew that prayer was important, and as I hadn't yet experienced the prayer meeting, I naturally felt obliged.
Twenty minutes into the prayer meeting I was kicking myself for giving in so easily. The warning signs were there from the beginning as Jasper is clearly the main speaker on a Sunday. Well, at least after Derek - our church believed in what was called 'body ministry.' We used to joke that it would be great to have a massage in the middle of the service, but what it really meant was providing time in the service for people in the congregation to contribute – well, to contribute pretty much whatever they wanted.
There was no set format so during the worship the band would play more quietly, or stop altogether, and whoever was leading the service through would ask if there were one or two people who would like to pray or who would like to share a word from God, and because there were only about a hundred and twenty adults it was small enough for

them to shout out from where they were, and boy, did Jasper shout. He was always first off the mark, well before anyone else could try to speak, he would start "THANKYOU GOD, HOW GREAT YOU ARE GOD, HOW GOOD HOW GREAT, HOW GOOD, WE LOVE YOU GOD," pause (still shouting) "I WAS READING TODAY ABOUT GOD'S LOVE, AND I WANT TO SAY I LOVE YOU GOD, AND I THINK GOD IS TELLING US THAT HE LOVES US TODAY, YES, DEFINITELY, GOD LOVES US, AND IF YOU'RE HURTING AND IN PAIN THEN GOD WANTS YOU TO KNOW YOU'RE NOT ALONE, THANK YOU GOD, GOD IS GOOD, YES, AMEN, AMEN, AMEN."

And believe me, that was just a taster of what we would get each week. It happened with such Swiss All-Bran regularity that we took to timing it: he had an average of two minutes talking and twenty seconds of 'amen.' Try saying amen over and over for twenty seconds and then you will understand. The latest betting stakes were for how many amens he would finish with. It's not that Jasper was intrinsically bad, or we were particularly mean, but his very presence inhibited me from ever daring to bring someone on Sunday – something we were encouraged to do regularly and something that most people seemed to do very irregularly!

Anyhow, I digress, back to the prayer meeting. Our church put huge emphasis on prayer: we prayed for everything and everyone entirely lifelessly in endless repetition.

We would come in to some 1980s horror music, or pan

pipes that blared out *Amazing Grace*, and sat in a circle. Jasper always put out forty chairs, even though he told me he had never seen more than twenty attend - apparently, God had said if he put them out, God would fill them. It reminded me of *Field Of Dreams*, the Kevin Costner movie, when the voice whispers 'if you build it, they will come...' It was a bit spooky but Jasper faithfully held out for his forty - and when Derek had suggested putting out just twenty, Jasper had loudly accused him of lacking faith and needing to pray more. Since then, no-one mentioned the chairs. They just sat empty every week.

Usually, the prayer meeting was attended by the lifers (those who faithfully felt it was their duty to attend) although they sat through at least half of the meeting with their heads in their hands, or their eyes rolling upwards, looking like they were about to fall asleep.

Except, of course, when Jasper prayed. When he prayed, everyone was awake. There were even rumours the people living next to the school had called the police one evening because of the noise level of what had sounded like an raving mentalist!

He would boom his prayer to heaven, repeat it twice and then fire it off once more for good luck, or so I thought. His favourite subject for prayer was revival. This involved a five minute solo rant on the state of the church and the need for more prayer and yes, Derek the pastor was sat beside him cringing!

So this time my response to the offer (or demand?) to join the prayer meeting was well prepared:

"I'm really sorry Jasper, I'm washing my hair."

And with that, I took off.

But I desperately wanted to attend church. Well, wanted to attend *a* church: but it had to be one that wasn't wallowing in itself. But, for want of a better option, and out of a duty and a desire for a difference, it was two weeks later, and I was back.

We were smack bang in the middle of the annual Evangelistic Week - it was the third day in and, by all accounts, this was shaping up to be like every other year: the diehards and lifers were out in force. You know, the ones who talk and talk and talk (and talk) of revival and, to be fair to them, are 'good people' (whatever that means) but are just caught in a time warp. To give them their dues, they do come out for the evangelistic week, but it's just they always look like another race that has landed from Mars - you know what I mean, they have that look that says I AM A CHRISTIAN, STEER CLEAR OF ME OR I WILL POUNCE!

In actual fact, they are always really pleasant, it's just that they've mastered that intense look and they seem to stare right through people, and they look stern all the time, whether they're in worship or listening to the preacher.

So here we were in the middle of the high street, singing our lungs out to *From The Rising Of The Sun* surrounded by polo-neck wearing, Bible-waving, foot-tapping, eye-darting Christians whom I had to call my brothers. It happened like this - someone down the other end of the street would hear the noise, seem initially interested, and continue walking down, staring to see what was going on and why forty people were huddled around a mini stage. As they drew closer, the scene would unfold rapidly and always in the same manner - their eyes would come to rest on the banner precariously held above the stage (getting this past the church Health and Safety monitors was a most difficult feat, "You know the banner could fall over and someone could die or be maimed by a sign that says, 'Jesus saves.'"Brilliant.)

As they saw the banner, heard the music, and saw the hand waving, you could visibly see the cloud parting and the realisation come that they had just walked into a Christian minefield - it was as if you could see their mouth drop open in slow motion and start to slowly shout noooooooooo, seeking any way to get out of this danger zone.

At this point we had prepared our Exocet missile - the evangelistic team, a group within the group, oh yes, the specialists. The evangelistic team comprised of ten people who would swoop to grab passers by, hand them a leaflet and by all means possible entice them into our resource centre (the creaky gazebo) to give them tracts and somehow in five minutes convert them, or at least get them to feel so pressured that they say they will come to church. Whether or not they do is never the point: the testimony is all in the fact they said they would.

I learnt this lesson just after the evangelistic week when Derek was sharing an amazing testimony from the front of church about how he had met a man called Roger who had an amazing past: he had been divorced, was a recovering alcoholic who had lost touch with his family and was now struggling with pornography, and how Derek had been able to pray for him and give him some appropriate literature (that caused a laugh...)

However, little did Derek know that on that very day, Roger was sat on the far end of the aisle on the back row - listening to his life story now being told to a hundred and fifty strangers. Worse was to come when Derek got the whole church to stand up to pray for this Roger, that he might come one day to church and find salvation and repent of his sins and be forgiven. By now, this man at the back had gone bright red and, looking extremely peeved, stood up and shouted an expletive that had something to do with not being into porn any more and stormed out muttering, "How could they? How could they?"

When approached by one of the ushers, he just started muttering, "I'm Roger, I'm Roger, now leave me the heck alone."After this incident, testimonies of this kind were moved to the prayer meeting, when they could guarantee only Christians and lifers would attend!

There's so much more that could be said about my experiences of church, but I won't go on. The purpose was to make you laugh and maybe make you feel a little embarrassed - I sure do. And yet we wonder why Christians get a bad press and the majority of society would not want to be tagged with the label!

It's a story of a church doing church for church with *little to no impact* on the society and community in which it lives, but goes on convincing itself that with a little more prayer, with more fasting, and with more exposition that the world will change.

I'm not so sure. I think it more likely that spiritually fat people will get fatter and simultaneously more satisfied that at least they are doing their little bit. To use the *Titanic* analogy, they are the people bucketing water over the side as the ship slowly sinks, telling everyone not to worry, they have it covered and - hey! - if that doesn't work then surely God Himself will come to the rescue!

Is anyone else feeling extremely embarrassed at what we have done with God's church?

Come on now, be honest with ourselves - there's hope if we are honest.

WE have made Him the LAUGHING STOCK of the nation.

In the final analysis...

Awareness always precedes action. For example, if you are eating lunch and you accidentally smear mayonnaise around your face, what do you do?
Nothing, until someone tells you, and then what do you do? Take action and remove it. Or, let me come at it from another angle:

> Here I am! I stand at the door and knock.
> If anyone hears my voice and opens the door, I will come in and eat with him, and he with me.
> *(Revelation 3v20, NIV)*

The statement above is addressed to a community of believers. It's a picture of Jesus knocking on the door of one of His own churches: He is **outside** the church although the church seems to think He is inside. I guess that's the picture I have for many churches in the UK today: they are still functioning and doing church, just without Jesus!

Jesus has left the building a long time ago and we haven't even noticed!

God is the most aware Being ever, and cannot be at home in unawareness, self-delusion or unreality; we have chosen not to have awareness, nor to have a reality check nor a truthful look at the situation. So much so that Jesus is now on the outside looking in, trying to attract people's attention to the fact He is outside. The good news is that it only takes one person to stand up and acknowledge Jesus' voice, or to put it another way, to accept Jesus' reading of the church's real condition. To 'open the door' means to admit the situation, to become aware of it and to want to do something about it. We cannot make a start on putting things right with the church until we have the awareness that there is something fundamentally wrong with it in the first place, that a little bit of tinkering won't make any difference.

God has already spoken on this:

> *For if God did not spare the natural branches, He will not spare you either. Consider therefore the kindness and sternness of God: sternness to those who fell, but kindness to you, provided that you continue in His kindness. Otherwise, you also will be cut off. And if they do not persist in unbelief, they will be grafted in, for God is able to graft them in again.*
> *(Romans 11 v21-24, NIV)*

Unless we recognise where we really are and how dire the situation really is, we won't make the changes necessary to not only keep the church alive, but flourishing and strong. Paul's message in Romans 11 is don't take it for granted that God will always be with you. The picture I've tried to paint suggests He's already moved on a long time ago as

He looked across a **stubborn, weak, hard of hearing church that stopped representing Him years, decades, maybe even centuries ago.**

My point is, like the last moments on the *Titanic*, the time for alterations and facelifts is over: **the time for wholesale, massive and complete change is here.** It's only the story of the last two thousand years that at some point, God looks to His church to change, adapt and become relevant again for a new generation.

This is that moment.

This is that time.

Part 2: Vision, Tips, Tools & Strategies

Firstly, and most importantly, a **shout out** to **leaders...**

To lead is to give vision, to take people on a journey, to get people excited, to walk people up the mountain, to deliver, deliver, deliver - and if you're not up for it, then don't go for it. (Who knows, that nugget might stop good people becoming bad leaders!)

Never forget that what is basic should remain basic. We should not make a big thing of prayer, worship and Bible-reading. These are the foundations on which the Church is built so once they are in, move on!

> *Therefore let us leave the elementary teachings about Christ and go on to maturity, not laying again the foundation of repentance from acts that lead to death, and of faith in God.*
> *(Hebrews 6 v 1, NIV)*

Do you get it? Try the Message:

> *So come on, let's leave the preschool finger painting exercises on Christ and get on with the grand work of art. Grow up in Christ. The basic foundational truths are in place: turning your back on 'salvation by self-help' and turning in trust toward God.*

RANDOM QUESTION
Why would a leader ever see someone for counselling, or anything else for that matter, if that person isn't reading his or her Bible and praying regularly?

Basics, as any primary or secondary school teacher knows, are things that should be taught and caught immediately, not things that are majored on throughout your school or church years. Everyone should be doing these things - just read the first part of Acts!

For dying churches, everything revolves around the basics. But just as GCSE or A-Level students will not achieve great results while focusing on their ABCs or their 123s, the church will not achieve while focusing on its basics.

Let's start at the beginning...

This is what the Lord Almighty says: "These people say, 'The time has not yet come for the Lord's house to be built.'" Then the word of the Lord came through the prophet Haggai: "Is it a time for you yourselves to be living in your panelled houses, while this house remains a ruin?"

Now this is what the Lord Almighty says: "Give careful thought to your ways. You have planted much, but have harvested little. You eat, but never have enough. You drink, but never have your fill. You put on clothes, but are not warm. You earn wages, only to put them in a purse with holes in it.

"Give careful thought to your ways. Go up into the mountains and bring down timber and build the house, so that I may take pleasure in it and be honoured," says the Lord.

"You expected much, but see, it turned out to be little. What you brought home, I blew away. Why?" declares the Lord Almighty. **"Because of my house, which remains a ruin, while each of you is busy with his own house."**

(*Haggai 1 v 2-9, NIV*)

This paints a pretty clear picture - **just where is our focus?** What are we building, and how well are we building it?

Of the millions of us who do attend church every week, how many of us are **builders**? How many of us are not just attending, being blessed and getting what we can, but giving, and giving to God's house?

Haggai's message is simple: put God first. Put His house first. **Put the local church first.** Commit to Him. Give time to Him, bring your creativity, time, energy, skills - your life to Him. It's like Haggai holds up a scale to us: at one end is your life, and the other end is God's house.

Where are you on this scale in terms of your focus?

Are you more focused on you and building your life, or on God's house?

Haggai makes a very clear point that when we put our focus on God's house, everything else follows. Jesus said the same, when He said in Matthew 6 v33, *"Seek first the Kingdom and all other things shall be added to you."* (The all other things, in the context of that chapter, are food, clothing and shelter - everything we *need* to do life.)

My point is that the very first thing we need to do is commit each day to living for God and to building His house. It's not something you can do once and then leave, it's something we need to do every day.

Again, as Jesus put it, take up your cross daily and follow Him. **Contribution follows commitment.**

You need to make this commitment.

If we're honest with ourselves, it's the same old story -

twenty percent of the people doing eighty percent of the work. Everyone tells me that's normal, that's the way life is.

Well, I'm not so sure. I think God called everyone in His kingdom to commit, to work, to give their all. Imagine churches that turn this principle on its head and have eighty percent of the people committed. Just imagine what we could achieve!

Imagine the giving levels!

Imagine the people we could reach!

Sounds like a **revolution**. Sounds like a **revival**.

Time For The Good News

There are some individual churches which are changing and not before time! We have been stuck in a time warp but if we can change fast enough then we will not be doomed. The only thing that holds us back is our own mindsets – how fast we can change the beliefs that have held us back.

A big mindset that needs to change is "we've tried all this change stuff before in the 1970s, and '80s, and '90s, so why do we think it will work this time?" This mindset is most prevalent in the over 40s who have become frighteningly cynical. They almost look with condescension on young people as the young work hard and foolishly believe that they can change the situation.

So here comes a major piece of wisdom: the situation will only change when all the generations in individual churches come together with the same vision and passion and they start practising what I am talking about in this book.

It's that simple – what makes this book different is that everything in it has been put into practice in my church, with unbelievably massive results! So there it is – apply the information in this book and we can change the world.

But if you read it, analyse it, dissect it and then do nothing with it, you will join the ranks of other leaders and Christians who have become the biggest blockage to their own vision to see a relevant, credible and powerful church in today's society.

Change is good, change can save us from oblivion, but change is hated in church (remember: old is good, tradition is good.)

So we need to challenge everything -
> why do we do this?
> why do we do it that way?
> is there a better way?
> does it have any purpose anymore?
> is it relevant to this generation?

Check out God in Psalm 50: He said I don't want the sacrifice of animals but a sacrifice of praise – namely, He wanted change.

God has sent His answer and we are seeing it in what is being termed **new breed churches** emerging across the nation, but they are not emerging fast enough or numerously enough to turn things around.

We need massive action or 'good' churches will continue to struggle on and will continue to fail.

We've already seen why: because of poor leadership, because of a lack of fundamental change in thinking and through sheer stubbornness. At the current rate of decline, practising Christians will soon form less than five per cent of the UK population, less than those practising Islam. Then why not be a Muslim nation?

The answer lies with churches that have strong leadership (not shepherding, nor stupid, but strong) with clear vision and a hunger and passion for God, built with adaptability and driven by a love for the lost.

SO WHAT DOES THE CHURCH NEED TO DO TO NOT

SINK

BUT RISE UP AND BE ALL IT WAS MEANT TO BE AGAIN?

Get A New Map.

God's big word for this time is: it's time to get a new map.

Say you're going on a trip to Leeds and you take your map of Leeds, but when you get there it doesn't make sense - the roads you thought should be there weren't, or had different names, and where there was meant to be a road it was now a dead end, and where there was meant to be no road but a park there was now a new housing estate. You look at the map and realise it was a map of Leeds for 1976, not today.

Or say you are going on a trip to London with a friend and you have both bought a map to help you get around. But before you have even set off you are disagreeing - they say that the bridge is two streets down, you say there is no bridge...the argument goes on and on until you decide to part ways!

The point: you both had maps of London, but one was for today, and the other was for a few years ago - that's how quickly they get updated. The world changes constantly so we need to update our maps regularly.

So here is the thing - many of us are using maps that are not relevant for today.

Especially the 'good people' who are now in their fifties and sixties, who so believed for revival but have now themselves become a major stumbling block for growth and change as they try to maintain their map of 'doing' church - the problem is that their map is for 1986, or 1996, or even last year, but not for **today**!

They keep getting lost, or worse, imposing their map on today's generation. How often do we go to someone else's church and try to navigate through it? The only thing is, we are using our map and not their church's map - we look for communion, reflective worship, spontaneous prayer, falling over or whatever, but the thing is it's the wrong map.

The trouble is, rather than see this, we get frustrated and angry, or worse, say that they are not really going for it, or that they are not scriptural, or whatever it might be.

To get the most out of a church you need to get the same map that the church leaders are using and get to know your way around, otherwise you'll get frustrated and disillusioned as you use your map to navigate around that church. If this isn't the map you want to use, then thank goodness for choice and variety! I know some people feel that the number of denominations and variety of churches is a negative, but I don't - I see it as another of God's gifts, recognising that although we all follow the same God, we outwork it in very different ways. Just look at the number of races in the world - how dull it would be if there was only one? So the responsibility is on church leaders to get an updated map that is easily followed by the people in your area today.

So you may be asking what is the map for today?
And hear that - a map for *today*.

Some things to look out for on today's map...

1. Empowering Leadership
High quality, growing churches are led by people who motivate, equip, coach and support their emerging leaders as they grow in their roles and increase their skills and anointing. They are leaders of leaders.

2. Letting People Do What They're Good At
Serving in an area we're good at does a lot to create happy, contented Christians, and is a much more effective way of using people's skills and gifts. Often in church, the minister or leader does everything and so fantastic people with great abilities can be sat with masses of untapped potential. If the church began to release its people in their area of strength, we would see some phenomenal results.

3. Passionate Spirituality
Zeal for the cause of Christ is critical to church health. The church needs a lot more people who are passionate and excited, with a 'can do' attitude, who are always smiling, always hungry for the next meeting, who arrive early and have to be kicked out at closing – who are raving fans of the church.

4. Functional Structures
Healthy, growing churches continually evaluate their structures and modify or eliminate them to ensure that they do not inhibit the church from accomplishing its purpose.

5. Inspiring Worship Services

Worship styles are irrelevant in determining whether or not churches experience healthy growth. Services can be targeted towards believers or non-believers, or be contemporary or traditional. The real issue is the impact the worship service has on the lives of those participating. Do they enjoy being in worship? Is the atmosphere conducive to experiencing God?

6. Smaller Groups

Smaller groups multiply as they meet the real needs of people. Moving beyond mere discussion of a biblical text, these groups enable believers to apply biblical principles in daily life and provide a forum for friendship. The larger a church becomes, the more crucial the role of smaller groups in maintaining healthy growth. These smaller groups can be cell groups, purpose groups, teams - it doesn't matter, as long as they're not talking shops or pity-parties but have a clear purpose and are active.

7. Need-oriented Evangelism

Being a Christian doesn't automatically make you an evangelist. In fact, the title evangelist has become a real barrier to Christians sharing their faith, as everyone looks to those with the 'gift' of evangelism to do all this. Everyone needs to be active in sharing their faith and to be **bringers**, people who bring their friends and family to church events, and not just rely on the keenest or the 'evangelists' to do it for them. We also need to ask if we are serving the needs of our community. Do we help mums and toddlers? Or run community action, house clearing or street cleaning schemes? Is there youth and kids work? Whatever it might be, if your community needs it, do you do it?

Great Relationships

Churches experiencing high quality growth have people who look out for each other and enjoy being together. This is vital to look out for on your map, that as you look across the church, do you see people genuinely enjoying being together, or are people rushing off as soon as the event is over? Are new people being included and feeling relaxed enough to stick around?

Almost as soon as the map is written, it will begin to change and will need updating. This is no different to the Acts of the Apostles - go read, or re-read it, and see how many times Paul had to deal with Peter's map and give him a new one: look at everything on Gentiles, eating meat, worshipping together...it goes on and on.

The map is constantly updated to stay relevant.

LEADERSHIP

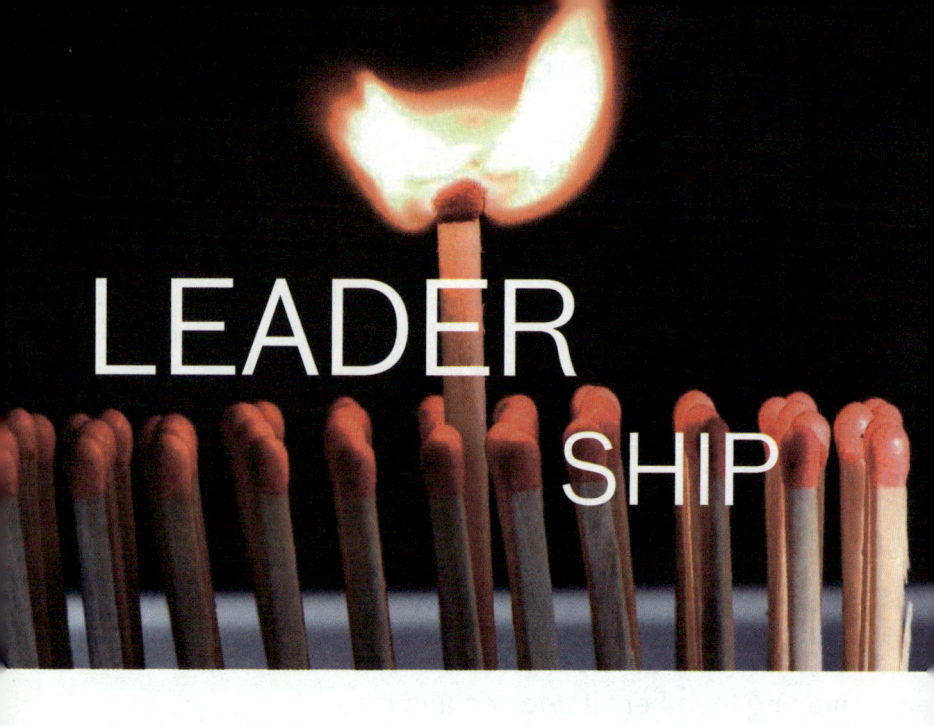

For too long now we have relied more on the 'ship' part of leadership – the institution, the title – rather than the 'leader' element, which is the skills and abilities that need time and effort in order to develop.

The number one reason for the current state of the church is its leadership. As in business, or football management, or in fact, anything, it is with the person at the top where responsibility ultimately lies.

Our leaders have a lot for which to answer. Have they feared change? Have they descended into making the people who are saved happy at the expense of those who are unsaved and dying? It seems like they see their role as a teacher and to keep the peace, to have an easy life. But there is a way forward, because God never leaves us without an answer.

A leader leads - it sounds basic, but how many bosses can you remember who have failed to lead? **A true leader is out ahead of others**, they are not necessarily the best at anything but nevertheless they are out ahead, **constantly changing themselves,** seeking self-improvement and are never satisfied.

In many ways they're extremely annoying, but they always have a clear sense of purpose and vision, they love a challenge and thrive with change and with new discoveries. They do a lot more than just teach: they are the main influence on a church. Ultimately, they understand they are building something bigger than just a few people, or even just a lot of people.

Everything about leadership has changed, it's been through a revolution, but I'm not sure the church has noticed.

Why does it seem like our leaders are so useless? You often look at them and think to yourself...no way, they can't be for real. Where is their fight, their passion, their conviction?

No wonder captains of industry, or politicians in power, or A-list celebrities don't come to church for their advice: they see most of its leaders, and they run a mile.

I was recently talking with a friend who is a successful businessman in London and he told me how he had been to church recently, and that he would never go again. He told me that the minister was not someone he could ever follow - he was weak, boring and a useless communicator, but like so many other identikit pastors, he was up there, at the front, telling everyone how he had felt the call.

That may be the case, but what was he doing to improve his abilities as a leader?

Nothing.

I have a theory that most leaders are 'good people,' but not actually leaders.

Even though it's plain to see that they're not cutting it, they are defended as 'good people.'

Stop that.
Stop that now.

Whether or not they are a good person is not the question. The Bible resounds with bad leaders who were good people - just look at the Pharisees.

These people who lead, they will always be good people. But we should not watch idly by and accept good people giving bad leadership, so ask yourself:

RANDOM QUESTION

What do you do when you are in a situation where your leader is a good person but a bad leader?

Or, to put it another way, what's more important - loyalty to a good person, or God's house?
Is it loyalty, or truth?
Is it good people, or God's house?

When leadership fails, I believe there are two ways to respond. Firstly, to appeal to a higher authority and be honest with them about what is happening. Secondly, if your feedback is not received and the situation doesn't change, and the leader does not or will not make the changes to become a better leader, than you need to peacefully withdraw from under their authority.

If people in leadership are willing to make the changes, then there are six things that leaders who want to be awesome need to be doing, or just plain need to be. Firstly,

New Breed Leaders are...

VISIONARIES

The word "vision" is overused and has lost much of its meaning and appreciation. We often think of it in terms of companies providing the obligatory vision statement which its employees are detached from or churches which produce a vision or mission statement which sound the same as all the others.

All well and good, but it has lost its power as people become sceptical as to whether the vision will ever happen. The term has just become a sound bite. In a world where "vision" has been used so often (and too often inappropriately), what does it mean to be truly visionary?

Real vision and true visionaries lift us out of the mundanity of everyday life and into the higher realms of imagination and possibility. As Agape International founder and spiritual director Rev. Dr. Michael Beckwith said, **"a visionary helps awaken and direct the inner strength of the people."**

Visionary leaders can't stand the norm if the norm is mediocre – or worse, restrictive or sub-standard.

They are fanatical about painting a picture of a better future and, most importantly, people's place within that. **They take what is in the future and bring it into the present**, turning people on, invigorating and stirring people for a greater possibility, stirring them towards a greater future.

I know it's clichéd, but think of Winston Churchill in 1940, think about Martin Luther King, think of Billy Graham – yes, think of Jesus Christ. All of them leaders who truly encompassed the role of visionaries, and with spectacular results.

New Breed Leaders are

ACTION MEN

You can never stand still around a leader who is an action man - there's just too much going on. If you find yourself in the world of a real leader, you will suddenly find yourself in the middle of a pragmatic revolution.

Leaders understand that if you're on the field of play, you better be doing something. Leaders know that to make things happen means taking action.

Vision is great, but only if it is acted upon.

So would all the action men please stand up?

Jesus was one of the busiest men the world has ever known - always doing.

So many leaders are scared of this, they talk about quiet time and taking time out to think and reflect - which is all well and good, but let's look at when Jesus took His time out:

> One of those days Jesus went out to a mountainside to pray, and spent **the night** praying to God. When morning came...
> (*Luke 6 v12-13, NIV*)

So Jesus always took time out, but He was selective and chose carefully - most of His time was in action! If you feel that not much is going on at your church, try doing something: take action.

New Breed Leaders are

ANGRY OPTIMISTS

If you spend time around a great leader, you will find that more often than not, they are driven by something that really gets them angry. This is because they have vision and imagine the world to be a better place, and because it is not, they get angry.

The present irritates them: they want **more, faster, quicker.**

Leaders need to see success and achievement! That's what they live for, and if they don't see it soon enough, they get angry. Look at your boss at work who gets mad over a lack of success or achievement: it motivates us all.

There is a need in the leader to make success happen, and they get angry if it does not. This is then twinned with optimism so the **fire in their belly** is partnered with **a smile on their face!** Complicated creatures, leaders!

Leaders, despite the anger, understand that not everything will go their way and that's when they learn to smile. They'd be naïve to think that reality will always be what they want, that's why they need to be flexible and adaptable, and they need to exude confidence and hope in the future no matter what comes their way.

It makes people focus and not go into self-pity mode, which is another thing that is destroying the church, and destroying people across the planet. A leader's confidence spreads into others: their very presence helps steady the course. Think about a difficult situation at work: when a leader turns up, you are relieved, and you trust in them to sort the situation out.

New Breed Leaders

MAKE MISTAKES

Leaders will make mistakes, and they don't try to hide them. In fact, they openly admit them, because they understand that to achieve anything great will mean trying something new, and that means making mistakes. Remember, Winston Churchill was a failure at the Admiralty, but he went on to become a great leader, and a great man.

We live in turbulent times as a church and leaders will have to make decisions and take action that will not always produce good results: in fact, they could make a total mess. This is something I feel we're all familiar with!

Messing up goes hand in hand with taking action. In these dire times, the church faces bold, big and major action. This may lead to massive failure, but as David Kelley (founder of IDEO Product Design) said, **"fail faster, succeed sooner."**

I guess what I'm trying to say (and perhaps badly) is that there is a **massive and unbelievable lack of great leaders in the church today**.

I know there are faithful ministers and compassionate pastors - in fact, we seem to have them in abundance - but that's not what I'm talking about here.

Back to my analogy of the sinking *Titanic*. When people first boarded the *Titanic*, the leadership was calm, helpful, relaxed and focused on the needs of the people. After the *Titanic* hit the iceberg, the leadership had to change. They were still focused on the people, but it would have felt very different: they had to be more directive, more forceful, and a heck of a lot clearer on the vision they had.

The point I'm trying to make is that because the context had changed, it required them to change. As you look at the world today, the context is so different to the one it was ten years ago, let alone fifty years ago, and yet it seems that the leadership style is still in the context of half a century ago - a delusion that we are fine, that lots of people still come to church, that we still have influence and that being hot and excitable is somehow undesirable.

Yet we've seen in the pages of this book - never mind in the myriad of statistics to back it up, nor the stacks of personal testimonies in agreement – that we are a dying breed, and dying at an incredible rate, too. My firm belief is that there is no guarantee that God won't let us go all the way to the wall - it's happened before, and we're told that it will get a lot worse too!

We need a massive change from ministers and pastors who couldn't honestly say they were the kind of leaders described above. **It's not an inherently bad thing that they're not. But it is a bad thing if they choose not to become better leaders.** We need church leaders to take on the characteristics of the type of leader who understands the 'sinking-ship' context and have an appropriate leadership style for the current time.

New Breed Leaders

DEVELOP OTHER LEADERS

John Maxwell has written libraries on this so I don't want to reinvent the wheel. In fact, I suggest you look at buying Maxwell's *Developing the Leaders Around You* if you've not come across this. The point that I want to make here is that the leader has to become the *Number One Talent-spotter* in the church – they should spend their time searching, hunting down and sniffing out possible future leaders.

One of their roles in the church is to not only do this themselves but to train others to do the same. Think of Jesus walking by the shores of Lake Galilee and spotting the raw talent of Simon Peter, James and John. Here is the crux: the talent that you spot won't be the finished article and will probably look geeky, odd, awkward, obnoxious, ragged and utterly ill-disciplined - in fact, everything other than what you'd want to find on a leadership team.

But our job as leaders is to take that raw talent and develop it, like Peter from Simon. It takes time and it will cost you, and the cost will likely be more than time and effort. The cost could also include losing friends who think you are mad for hanging out with the fringe of your church or giving time to the group that's not the in-crowd.

But you will keep going because you know, just like Jesus, that there's a Peter in Simon, there's a rock hidden in the reed, a talent in the timid and strength in the weak.

At the moment, most churches look for one thing: a safe pair of hands to oversee and lead the church. What's wrong with this is that they are in the wrong position - they shouldn't be leaders, they should be in a position to take care of people! So why not use them in the area they are good at where they will outwork their role safely and bring in a dynamic leader to oversee the direction of the church?

Because there is nothing safe about church leadership: we are called to take up our cross daily, to take risks. Think of Paul's life, think of him talent-spotting Timothy, taking a risk on a young guy who was timid and shy but seeing past that and finding within Timothy something that he wanted to develop!

KNOW YOUR OUTCOME

Once real leadership is in place, the next step is to know your outcome or destination – to define precisely what it is you want. It might shock you to know that God has a plan for the universe -

> *Long, long ago He decided to adopt us into His family through Jesus Christ. (What pleasure He took in planning this!) He wanted us to enter into the celebration of His lavish gift-giving by the hand of His beloved Son. Because of the sacrifice of the Messiah, His blood poured out on the altar of the Cross, we're a free people - free of penalties and punishments chalked up by all our misdeeds. And not just barely free, either. Abundantly free! He thought of everything, provided for everything we*

could possibly need, letting us in on the plans He took such delight in making. He set it all out before us in Christ, a long-range plan in which everything would be brought together and summed up in Him, everything in deepest heaven, everything on planet earth. It's in Christ that we find out who we are and what we are living for. Long before we first heard of Christ and got our hopes up, He had His eye on us, had designs on us for glorious living, part of the overall purpose He is working out in everything and everyone.
(*Ephesians 1 v5-12, MSG*)

Once this plan is in place, it is time for action - otherwise your desires will always remain dreams. We must take the types of actions we believe will create the greatest probability of producing the result we desire. The actions we take do not always produce the results we desire, so the next step is to get and receive feedback to recognise how successful we are. Using the results we are getting we must note, as quickly as possible, if they are taking us closer to our goals or further away from them. We should always be aware of what results we are getting from our actions, whether it be from our conversations or from our daily habits in life.

If we're not getting the results we want, we need to learn what results our actions have produced and learn from them to fully learn the lesson. And then we must take the next step – to develop the flexibility to change our actions and behaviour until we get what we want.

If you look at successful people and successful churches,

you will find that they followed these steps. They started with a target, because you'll find it impossible to hit a target if you don't have one. They took action and they kept adjusting and changing their behaviour until they found what worked.

The opposite of this is the people who always seem lost in a fog of confusion, who are constantly trying one thing, then another, twisting
          and
        turning,

up   and   _{down,}

left
        and
                  right.

They seem to be on one road, then wham! Swap roads. The diagnosis?

They don't know what they want, and as we all know, you can't hit a target if you don't know what it is.

Going Wild and Dreaming Big

It's all about using your imagination to dream into the kind of church you want to create and build.

This does need to be done in a structured and focused way - you'll need plenty of resources and a place where you can allow your creativity and imagination to flow!

This is about setting goals and deciding on the outcomes that you want for your church.

You are going to create a destiny, a future state that you will passionately move toward - and it doesn't matter if this is the first time you have done this or the fortieth!

Just don't limit yourself, the Bible says that all things are possible (take a second on that: **all things**) for those who are called - God wants us to dream big, He created us to dream big.

They say that the universe is still expanding, that it is still being created - ponder that for a moment. It is the greatness of God that He is still building the universe, so now when you think about His church, don't minimise it, don't shrink it down, let's be bold and audacious, and let's dream big!

If you KNEW you COULDN'T FAIL, what would you attempt?

FOUR TIPS
FOR DREAMING BIG

1. State your goal in positive terms and verify it is Godly.
*Say what it is you want to happen. We often talk about what we **don't** want and then these negatives become our goals. Project into the future the consequences of achieving your goal - will it be one that benefits people and honours God?*

2. Be specific.
There's no need to waffle here and talk vaguely about growth or increasing the finances. The more detail you create, the more you will empower yourself to create the desire. Always give yourself an end date to work towards. We need to be so much more specific than just a bigger church, or more involvement from people, or better prayer, greater worship and increasing finances. Once you have consciously decided what you specifically want, you are in a better position to get it.

3. Evidence the achievement.
Imagine the future. Know how you will feel and what you will see and hear when the goal is achieved. Before something happens in the external, it must happen internally to us. Whenever we get a clear internal picture of what we want, it programs our minds and bodies to achieve that goal. Successful sportsmen are renowned for using PMA (Positive Metal Attitudes) to visualise achievements and bring them into their world.

Be in control.
You own the goal and you kick it off, it must not be dependent upon other people achieving, or on them changing themselves for you to be happy.

> **"Where there is no vision, people perish."**
> (Proverbs 29 v18)
> (Yes, it's oft-quoted. But it doesn't stop the wisdom of the Bible being any less true, or any less appropriate for this time.)

The people are desperate, dying for lack of leaders willing to set audacious goals that will cost but are 100% pure vision. The people are perishing as churches say that they would like a few more people to come to church or a bit more money to help the building fund and maybe one or two people to come to the prayer meeting and possibly some help running a youth club – but this isn't having goals and knowing your outcomes, this is about weak and pathetic leadership that has lost its focus and its desire!

Churches which are successful have become so because they know where they are going and they are clear about it. They dream the future and then move toward it.

It's fun dreaming into what we want, and then going for it! Even if we fail, let's fail TRYING rather than not trying at all!

Remember the parable of the talents?

Attracting the next generation

We all talk about this, think about this, and pray about this...but remember, faith is nothing without action.

Faith without corresponding action is just hot air and hot air just makes blah blah blah statements...

With one voice, the church proclaims:

"We want the young people to go far in our church, blah blah blah..."

"We need to move out of the way to let the young people go past us, blah blah blah..."

"We need to change with the times and recognise the next generation do things in a different way, blah blah blah..."

"We want to pass the baton on, blah blah blah..."

"Let's allow the young people to lead the service once a month, blah blah blah..."

And with another voice, the church complains...

"We don't like this modern, loud music."

"Young people need to learn and wait their turn, it's about wisdom and longevity."

"Young people make rash decisions and can't be relied upon."

"Young people need time to develop and mature."

"Young people need to know their place and respect their elders."

The people making these statements can block empowering the next generation.

FOR GOD'S SAKE, BE HONEST AND ADMIT IF THIS IS YOU. IF YOU HAVE TO, ASK SOMEONE. BECAUSE IF IT IS, YOU NEED TO CHANGE, AND TO DO THAT, YOU'LL NEED TO

DISTURB YOUR WORLD.

Choose to disturb your world.

Make the decision to disturb your world, to turn yourself upside down if necessary, to do whatever it takes at whatever cost to yourself. Disturb your world, and risk losing friends, gaining enemies, being misunderstood, misquoted, laughed at and ridiculed.

I've watched as one leader made the choice to disturb his world at the cost of his reputation and most of his ways of 'doing' church, and ended up winning the next generation.

He could have won the argument when the next generation told him that his way of doing church was failing them: he could have told them they were unsound biblically and also naïve and inexperienced, but he chose to listen to their hearts, to their passion for change and to their desire to be part of a church that was winning their generation.

It meant that the leader had to turn his world **UPSIDE DOWN** and find new ways of doing things, throwing out tried and tested ways, going with new songs, speeding things up, finding new comedy, using new activities and changing his thought patterns. However, none of this would have been possible had he not made the decision personally that, no matter what was thrown his way, he would disturb his world and keep changing.

Now for those of you who have got nervous and are worried that I am talking about throwing the baby out with the bath water – stop worrying!

Of course this generation knows more than the next and has better ways of articulating themselves. Of course they know more about the Bible, more about people and more about what the over forties like. Of course they know what has worked well in the past but **that's not the point.** This generation does have a few things that the emerging generation needs, but to be brutally honest, it's not much.

How do I know? Because the apostle Paul said it best:

> *No, dear brothers and sisters, I am still not all I should be, but I am focusing all my energies on this one thing: Forgetting the past and looking forward to what lies ahead.*
> (*Philippians 3 v 12-13, NLT*)

Hear it direct from Paul: "I am still not all I should be." So where should we look to be influenced and shaped? "Forgetting the past and looking forward to what lies ahead." Should we be shaped by the generation from the past which is disappearing, or from the emerging generation which is becoming the future?

You need to have an honest look across your church and see the picture as it is, not as you want it to be. Then, do some percentages. How many in your church are under thirty? How many are in the 11-18 bracket? Then, if you're really brave, ask some questions of the young people:

What's good about what we do at our Sunday service?
What could we improve and make better?
How could we attract more young people?

How could we involve you more?
What could we change?
How can we make it more accessible to your friends?
What would instantly attract new people?
What is good about what we currently do outside of the Sunday event?
What should we keep and what do we need to lose?

Once you have asked the questions then **take a risk** and **implement** some of the findings.

Don't just do nothing with them or else you'll lose the next generation!

The Power of Ideas

The truth is that today, more than ever, the biggest power is the power of an idea. There are people who see what exists and believe there's a creative way to shatter reality and make an extraordinary new reality. Even in politics, the people being groomed the most to become movers and shakers are those who appear to be idea factories.

In the next generation of church, we have to stop being afraid of new challenges like relativism, postmodernism, apathy, fragmentation, materialism, pluralism and stop seeing other ideologies (Islam, Buddhism) as bullets that will be aimed at our faith and destroy us. Rather, these should be seen as new ways to extend Christianity's powerful message.

The next generation must rise up and become **change insurgents**, people who will stop at nothing to shape, change and define the church. If it is left to the fading generation the situation will become very dangerous but why couldn't the current and the emerging work together?

We all know why...**FEAR**, the fear that somehow the emerging generation will compromise the truth or lose a few from the silver-haired brigade or be so radical as to actually reach the generation and cause a whole new problem – unbelievers in the church!

So Let's Take Risks!

In a fearful world, the ultimate weapon is fearlessness.

My advice: take chances, but do it properly.

Doing something which has never been done before, bending some rules, 'going public', investing in a new program or service, working across boundaries, and trusting the emerging generation...these are examples of risks that change agents need to and MUST take in order to achieve their goals.

Story Time!

About three years ago, I took the first steps in disturbing my world. I asked myself 'what's possible?' At the time, I was earning a very good salary, had a nice house, was happily married, felt strong in my spiritual life and was the youth leader of a local church where fifty or sixty youth attended. Everything was fine and I was content, but there was something inside of me asking, 'Is this it? Is there more?'

I began to wonder what was possible. Is it possible to double my earnings in a year and to give more? Is it possible to grow a youth group to hundreds and to see a church have a major influence on a city? Is it possible that there is so much more out there that I haven't even begun to imagine or experience?

Asking these questions stirred something up inside of me. We all believe that God has come to give us an abundant life (John 10v 10) and we wheel this scriptural nugget out at certain points to remind us that we are called to an abundant life, but as I looked at my life, I wasn't sure I was living abundantly.

I felt like I was living a middle-class life and I wasn't sure if that was scriptural or Godly. I had bought into the culture of middle-class comfort, rather than living God's life and all He has for me. I had a nice life, enough money for a holiday once a year and a decent car, but there was something growing in me, a feeling that God had more.

This led to me leaving my comfortable job. At the time, I was working closely with a number of senior directors at a major multinational company, and they told me plainly that I had two choices. Firstly, I could leave, and I might not be successful because I was still too young to set up my own business. Secondly, I could be fast-tracked so that at some point in the next ten years, I would reach director level with a six figure salary.

I found it appealing, really appealing, but still inside of me something was saying "is that it?" and that's even after talking about earning a six figure salary. Still, I felt like God had more for me.

At the same time I went to the pastor of the church I was attending and asked him what his vision for the church was and where he saw the church in the next five years. He sat there, did some figures, talked about church statistics, looked at the mean and the mode, and finally decided he would love to be three hundred in the next five years.

I came away from that meeting depressed because I was looking for vision and for him to have that same spirit of abundance and belief in what was possible, but I found that lacking.

At a later meeting I remember him asking one of the leading youth workers what his vision was, the young guy said he saw the church becoming 10,000 - a huge church that would influence a nation. The leader looked at him with disbelief and pity, a wearisome pity like long ago he had had that same abundant spirit that believed that all things were possible and then he said to him, "but church statistics tell us that that is impossible."

Right there, he was squashing the youth leader's belief in what God could do and lowering it down to his own minimal expectation. It would have been amazing if he had said, "wow, what faith, I need some of that faith, pray for me because I want to believe for that again." He would have shown leadership, as well as courage and humility -

and inspired the young leader! We need a cause that's so big, so bold and so challenging that it is worth getting out of bed to achieve it. To this young youth leader, the vision of being a massive church was worth getting out of bed for! Think of Jesus saying to the disciples as He was going to heaven "go into all the world" - what a vision! That's a big, hairy audacious goal that's definitely worth getting out of bed for!

To finish the story, I took the bold step to leave my role at the corporate company and set up my own company doing business coaching with different companies in different sectors. In the first year of business on my own, I tripled my salary! So why is that important? Well, guess where a lot of the extra income went – straight back into the kingdom of God!

It took guts and boldness and a strong belief that there was more in store for me to step out. Fear could have easily stopped me, as it says in Proverbs "fear...will prove to be a snare." (*Proverbs 29 v25, NIV*) Yet all the time God had more for me, it just took me time to realise it, to get an abundance mindset! Let me go a little deeper...

Belief Systems

God needs to cut through our BS, our Belief Systems, which get in the way of us believing that He is abundant and wants us to live an abundant life.

So what is a belief system?

A belief is a single thought that we have spent time thinking upon until it has affected our general thinking. When we allow these thoughts to affect our general thinking, we have become slaves to a belief system. For example, think of someone you know who believes they are not confident, or not a good Christian, or are fat, or ugly - how did they get to that belief?

They repeatedly thought again and again, over and over, *I am useless*, or *I am ugly,* or *I'm not good with people* until it has become something they utterly believe – this is basic cognitive psychology.

The Bible puts it really clearly, "For as he thinks within himself, so he is."(*Proverbs 23v 7, NIV*) The more you think on something, the more you will believe it, and become it.

We have so many beliefs as a church that I'm no longer sure which are God's beliefs and which are our own.

We need to line up what we think with the ultimate truth - Jesus, who said "I am the way, the truth and the life."(*John 14 v6, NIV*) So if our beliefs develop by repeatedly thinking on a singular thought, what then do we need to think on to break them?

Let's take an example. My wife and are going out for a meal, she gets herself ready and comes down the stairs looking fantastic, but thinking in her head that she doesn't look good, she's thinking that she looks fat in her outfit. She asks me how she looks and I say, "Darling, you look gorgeous," and she says back to me, "I knew it, I knew I looked fat in this, I'm going to put on my other trousers!"

The point I'm trying to make is this, I could tell her anything - it wouldn't matter, because she has her own belief and nothing I say will change it. She needs to change her thoughts so that she believes that she looks good. It's a silly example but makes the point that what you think about, you will find.

Think on this – God has called us to an abundant life and will provide for us – and as you think on that, and find support in the Bible for it, you find yourself believing it and then you'll find abundance all over! That's because what we believe, we find.

Just think of your church. You have people who believe it is good and so when they go there on Sunday, they spot all the things that make it good – the worship, the passion, the young people, the preach, everything. Then think of those people in church who don't really like it – we all know they exist, their facial expressions give it away! They come to church and spot all the things they don't like about it, the loud drums, the riotous young people, the annoyingly modern message. You see: what we believe, we find.

When we **see** something differently,
we **do** something differently.
When we **do** something differently,
we **get** a different result.

God can tell us anything He likes, but unless we think on those things and allow them to become beliefs, we will always limit what is possible to our own level. We won't see what is possible because we won't allow ourselves to - we will only look for (and find) what we believe to be true!

> *How often they provoked Him in the wilderness, and grieved Him in the desert! Yes, again and again they tempted God, and **limited** the Holy One of Israel. They did not remember His power: the day when He redeemed them from the enemy.*
> *(Psalm 78 v40-42 NKJ)*

This sums up the story of the Old Testament. God chose a people and the people had to decide whether they would trust Him or not. They changed from putting their faith in Him to not trusting Him, and even though they had seen His power, they forgot about it. What had happened was that Israel had limited God - so the question I want to ask the church today is, have we limited God? Are we possessing all He has lined up for us?

We can limit God because of the beliefs we have about what is possible in our lives and in the church today, which is exactly what Israel had done. They had forgotten what God had done for them and so when trouble came, or enemies or even opportunities, they would often not respond - in other words, they limited what God wanted to do with them.

So the question remains, have we limited God? Is that the reason why the church is in the state it is in today?

Raising the temperature

A thermostat controls room temperature and it's like we have one for our lives and for our churches, too.

What has set the thermostats in your life or church? Is it fears, or faith in the promises of God? Let's turn our thermostat up and believe in God for more, turn it up just one degree. Now here's the thing with one degree: at 99 degrees centigrade water is extremely hot, but at 100 degrees water boils, and with boiling water, you get steam, and hundreds of years ago a genius came up with the idea that we could use steam to power an engine. This all came from raising the temperature by one degree: that's all that the church needs to do. By making a few small adjustments, we could raise the temperature and see massive results that affect a nation! One degree could tip us over the edge to receive all that God has for us. We can raise the temperature and trust the promises of God.

Limiting God is sad for you but worse for everyone else who was counting on you and needed you to bless them. Learn this now: someone is counting on you to bless their life.

I'm content with what I have now but I'm not satisfied. Paul told us to be content in all things - in other words, whatever context we're in, be content in it, whether we have much or little, we must learn to enjoy where we are.

But what he didn't say was that you had to settle and live there, that this is your context forever! Change your context, don't settle. Expect more and keep believing for so much more, for your own life and for the church. Contentment often leads to complacency, and then to apathy, and then spiritual weakness.

Keep striving for more!

You are what you believe

We've seen that you are what you believe, and that what you believe is possible determines the actions that you will take. We've seen that how you see the world will determine what you think is possible and therefore what action you attempt – and ultimately, what you will achieve.

See - Do - Get.

The type of job you have now has been set by the beliefs you have about the kind of job you are able to get. The amount of money you earn is set by what you believe you're worth – many people don't believe they are worth a nice car, so they don't drive a nice car. I had a friend come to me who has his own gardening business, I asked him how much he was charging and he told me £18 an hour. I asked him if he thought he was worth that, he said that he thought he was worth £25. So I asked him why he wasn't charging that – and he told me that he was worried people wouldn't pay it, which was a good point. He needed to test the market, so I recommended that he try to get some jobs for £25. He went for four jobs and got three of them - the market backed up his belief that he was worth more.

So what has set the thermostat of our life?

Do you believe that God wants you to prosper and have abundance? If you don't believe, you won't go for things and you will limit God. Trust what He can do for you and through you.

> "Look at the birds. They don't need to plant or harvest or put food in barns because your heavenly Father feeds them. And you are far more valuable to Him than they are."
> (Matthew 6 v26 NASB)

So my question to you is this: do birds have just enough trees and worms, or more than enough? Has God provided just enough worms for the birds, or a huge overwhelming abundance of worms so that the birds could never eat all of them? Are there just enough trees, or a massive abundance of trees of all shapes and sizes, so that there is more than enough foliage for the birds to build nests?

AND ARE WE NOT FAR MORE VALUABLE TO HIM THAN THEY ARE?

But what about areas that don't seem to have abundance, like Africa? To me, this is a prime example of poor stewardship, in fact every book, statistic and report indicates that Africa is rich with God's abundance in terms of natural resources. The issue isn't abundance, it is stewardship.

Abundance and MON£Y

"Instruct those who are rich in this present world not to be conceited or to fix their hope on the uncertainty of riches, but on God, who richly supplies us with all things to enjoy."
(1 Timothy 6 v17, NASB)

Here, Timothy is reminding us to recognise God's passion for us to have an abundance of all things to enjoy. He also reminds us of our need to remember what to put our faith in - not the abundance, but He who supplies the abundance.

It seems that most people don't accept abundance because they are worried about their heart and getting carried away or lost in their wealth. But that shouldn't be a reason not to accept abundance, it should be a reason to deal with your heart so that God can use you as an instrument of His abundance!

Most of the verses in the Bible about money are about dealing with your heart and getting your heart right.

Jesus lays the foundation of getting your heart right brilliantly in Matthew:

> *"No one can serve two masters; for either he will hate the one and love the other, or he will be devoted to one and despise the other. You cannot serve both God and money."*
> *(Matthew 6 v24, NIV)*

Have a look in Matthew 19 v16, and Luke 6 v38 - the point is Jesus gives us the key to unlock blessings. If we get our focus right, get our hearts right, and remember the giver and not the gift - then we are promised that abundance will come.

I believe that I have been born out of abundance because I came from a God whose "invisible qualities of abundance are written across the universe." (Romans 1) He is totally abundant and when I die, I am going back to abundance because Jesus called it paradise, and He has been preparing it for a very long time!

So we came from abundance, and we will go back to abundance. But the bit in the middle, the bit called my life, seemed to be lacking in abundance.

So, how do we get our focus right so we can start living abundantly now?

Detachment and desperation

We can make sure we get our focus right by applying Jesus' teachings to our lives. Jesus taught us detachment - which is not disinterest, for it is possible to be very detached and very determined. For example, if you apply for a job that you really want, you will do everything you can to get it – prepare thoroughly, dress well and arrive on time for an interview. At the end of the process, you go home and get on with your life - if you're hired, then you're happy, but if you're not hired, then you're still moving forward with your life, enrolling for further study and perfecting your application.

Disinterested people say,
"Who cares and why bother?"
Desperate people say,
"If I don't get this I'll die."

The more attached or emotional you are to things, the less control you have over them. Most people are very emotional about money and as a result they are out of control. Detachment is a major reason why the rich get richer. Jesus was teaching detachment, telling us we don't need money or possessions to be happy. Once He had taught that, guess what He could teach on - receiving abundance in all its forms! Jesus said don't store up treasures, He didn't say you couldn't have treasures!

Think about how much will it cost to reach the world.

£1? £1million? £1billion?

Who knows, but it will be a lot...think about how much it costs to run an Alpha, or to advertise on TV, or flyer a city, or fund hundreds of kids and youth workers...imagine a church full of well-paid workers who never have to worry about money as their focus is on reaching people and not money.

So isn't it interesting that the church has a major problem with money?

Why?

What are you afraid of?

Do you fear your own greed? Be honest with yourself - if it is, don't blame money, but work on your character.

When Jesus taught the Jews, He was realigning them as they had become unfocused. Look at money and prosperity in the light of realignment and you will see what Jesus is doing:

> *"Watch out! Be on your guard against all kinds of greed; a man's life does not consist in the abundance of his possessions."*
>
> *And He told them this parable: "The ground of a certain rich man produced a good crop. He thought to himself, 'What shall I do? I have no place to store my crops.'*
>
> *"Then he said, 'This is what I'll do. I will tear down my barns and build bigger ones, and there I will store all my grain and my goods. And I'll say to myself, "You have plenty of good things laid up for many years. Take life easy; eat, drink and be merry."'*
>
> *"But God said to Him, 'You fool! This very night your life will be demanded from you. Then who*

will get what you have prepared for yourself?'
"This is how it will be with anyone who stores up things for himself but is not rich toward God."
(*Luke 12 v13-21, NIV*)

Can you see it?

"Is not rich toward God."

The Jews understood prosperity as God had made success and prosperity part of His covenant with them, but what they needed realigning on was **purpose**.

They had forgotten their maker and kept all the riches for themselves when God had clearly taught them differently.

Notice that the problem isn't prosperity, growth, increase or abundance - the question is what we do with it, **how it is used.**

"The only people who think more about money than the rich are the poor." (Oscar Wilde)

The best thing you can do for the poor is not become one of them!

When we realise God is an abundant God, it will change us massively and inspire us to aim for so much more as a church. If we stop limiting God, set our thermostat up a bit and actually believe that all things are possible, then we will stop thinking small and stop thinking stingy and show the world how abundant our God is!

Still, some of you may have an issue with abundance. Let's deal with it.

The rich young ruler question:

As we read the passage of the rich young man in Matthew 19, we need to determine what his problem was. The trouble is, he was *motivated by scarcity and not abundance*. Mark 10 v17 says that the man ran up and knelt before Jesus and asked what he had to do to attain eternal life. The man seems eager to draw closer to God and was concerned about his eternal destiny. Jesus tells him to keep the commandments; the man replies that he has done this. The Gospel says, "Jesus, looking at him, loved him." Jesus loved him and wanted what was best for him, but Jesus senses that something is missing.

Like a surgeon detecting a malignant growth, Jesus wants to excise the cancer on this man's soul, which is his attachment to possessions.

The man didn't want to give up the possessions he had acquired which shows a total *lack* of abundance because abundant people understand that it involves giving and receiving and the **worst thing to do is hold on tightly to what you have.** It also shows that he trusted in his abundance, rather than in the abundant giver who provides it all – a major mistake!

But how much do we cling to our own possessions? We might be tempted to say, "Well, the man in the Gospel story is rich, and I'm not rich, so this Gospel is about Bill Gates or Warren Buffet, but it is not about me."

Wrong!

This Gospel passage *is* about you and me.

So now I hear someone say, "Jesus tells the man to sell what he owns, and give the money to the poor. Is Jesus telling me to give up all of my possessions?"
No.
Jesus is not against the ownership of private property, but the Gospel is desperately telling us to lessen our attachment to possessions. The Bible is very clear about God's chosen method to teach us this lesson: tithing, giving ten per cent to God, and keeping ninety per cent for yourself. If you do this you will take a very practical step of lessening your attachment to money.

It is time to get over YOUR problem with money. It is time to create an abundance mindset.

If we do this, the church is going to be taking in a lot of money - we need to be prepared to handle this. The Bible gives us the principle of giving and receiving.

> *"Do not be deceived: God cannot be mocked. A man reaps what he sows."*
> (*Galatians 6 v7, NIV*)

If you sow anger you will reap anger, if you sow hate, you will reap hate, if you sow love, you will reap love, sow money, reap money. It's a principle written into the universe, just like the principle of gravity, what goes up must come down!

God's spiritual law of giving and receiving can be summed up

Seed ➡ Time ➡ Harvest

Or, to make it clearer:

Effort ➡ Time ➡ Results

When the farmer goes out to sow, it takes effort to sow the seed. When we are sowing into our communities, it takes effort - effort to sow into the youth of the city and the kids and the business community. Sadly, so many churches are no longer willing to put the effort in, they would rather just turn up on a Sunday and maybe midweek and hope that people might come to know God.

If you look at all the most successful churches across the world, one characteristic they all have is that there is a lot of effort or sowing going on into lots of different people and lots of different areas. Most churches now cannot even be bothered to run events weekly, they struggle to get commitment from people beyond the Sunday and then wonder why they aren't seeing results.

We must grow what we sow and find people who are willing to sow into other people's lives, or as Jesus said:

> *"If anyone would come after me, he must deny himself and take up his cross daily and follow me."*
> *(Luke 9:23, NIV)*

Is the church willing to get sowing, give effort, get out of the house more than once a week on God's business, or will it settle for the current situation? Imagine if John Wesley had not been willing to put effort in! No revival, no life-changing, earth-shattering, God-anointed power encounter that rocked Great Britain. It's said he rode to the moon and back as he covered so many miles on horseback. Imagine, we have cars today and can't even be bothered to travel for ten minutes, in luxury, to help run a kids club, or a youth work, or to feed the poor or clothe the destitute.

We need to see movement again, to see energy and effort to stop the stagnation that is ruining the church! Most churches no longer have any movement, they just slowly and heavily do the few things they've been doing for the last hundred years!

Along with effort, we must also give time. If the farmer goes back to his seed after just a month, what will he find? Soggy seed. We must give endeavours a set amount of time and give them a chance to grow before we can reap.

> *Now this I say, he who sows sparingly will also reap sparingly, and he who sows bountifully will also reap bountifully. Each one must do just as he has purposed in his heart, not grudgingly or under compulsion, for God loves a cheerful giver....Now he who supplies seed to the sower and bread for food will also supply and increase your store of seed and will enlarge the harvest of your righteousness. You will be made rich in every way so that you can be generous on every occasion.*
> (*2 Corinthians 9 v6-7, NIV*)

God loves a cheerful giver because it mirrors Him. He gives cheerfully and He loves it when He sees us doing the same. It's like any parent who feels immense pride when they see their child doing something that they have taught them, and something that is good!

As we give, God will enrich us - in other words, He will restock us, so that we receive again and can keep on giving: the law of giving and receiving, as you give you shall receive!

When a farmer sows one seed into ground he doesn't expect just one seed back. Seed produces a stalk of corn which produces several ears of corn, with each ear producing many new seeds - all from the one seed that the farmer planted. This is the divine process of multiplication: God's principle says that those who give, get it back, and it will be multiplied!

> *"In everything I showed you that by working hard in this manner you must help the weak*

> and remember the words of the Lord Jesus, that He Himself said, `It is more blessed to give than to receive.'
> (*Acts 20 v35, NASB*)

It is more blessed to give than receive because when you give, you get back. You prosper greatly when you give because God enriches you to receive more – what a fantastic and exciting principle to try!

So, if this principle is true, does this apply to Jesus? We know He sowed His life into the world, so what did Jesus get back?

> *Therefore God exalted him to the highest place and gave Him the name that is above every name, that at the name of Jesus every knee should bow, in heaven and on earth and under the earth, and every tongue confess that Jesus Christ is Lord, to the glory of God the Father.*
> (*Philippians 2 v9, NIV*)

Or, to put the final nail in the coffin and put the principle to bed, look at Proverbs 3:

> *"Honour the Lord with your wealth, with the first fruits of all your crops; then your barns will be filled to overflowing, and your vats will brim over with new wine."*
> (*Proverbs 3 v9-10, NIV*)

The principle is there for all to see: trust God that when you sow, you will always reap something – and what you reap depends on what you sowed in the first place!

So what about when the economic outlook is not too good, or the finances aren't great, or you're all out of love and feeling annoyed or whatever the circumstances might be that would hold you back from sowing something - what then?

I want to challenge you to trust God's principle because that is true faith, to trust God when everything around you would tell you otherwise!

> *Be generous: Invest in acts of charity. Charity yields high returns.*
> ***(Ecclesiastes 11 v1, MSG)***

> *He who watches the wind will not sow and he who looks at the clouds will not reap. Just as you do not know the path of the wind and how bones are formed in the womb of the pregnant woman, so you do not know the activity of God who makes all things. Sow your seed in the morning and do not be idle in the evening, for you do not know whether morning or evening sowing will succeed, or whether both of them alike will be good.*
> ***(Ecclesiastes 11 v4-6, NASB)***

I can't tell you exactly how God's principles work, I just know that they do because I see the results! Like the pregnant women who gives birth, what this verse tells us to do is to trust God and sow all the time regardless of circumstance!

ABUNDANCE IS COMING

We need to act like abundance is on its way - James 2 shows us this principle when it talks about faith and corresponding action. We must take action based on our faith and then we need to claim the next step as a normal place to live.

Expect to win.

Expect people to be added to your church.

If you have sown and are sowing and you have given it time then expect to see results, look out for them - just as the farmer goes out into the field expecting to see his crop.

Finally, remove the roadblock of pessimism, excuses and a victim mentality to fully embrace the future:

> *Brethren, I do not regard myself as having laid hold of it yet; but one thing I do: forgetting what lies behind and reaching forward to what lies ahead.*
> (*Philippians 3 v13, NASB*)

The church is amazing at holding onto the past. It's time to let go of old ways that were suitable for the previous centuries but are redundant for the present and the future. Let's be like Paul and keep searching for what is next, **show adaptability on what isn't sacred and keep moving!**

What has set the thermostat for your church?

> "Jesus looked at them and said, "With man this is impossible, but with God all things are possible."
> (*Matthew 19 v26, NIV*)

What has set the thermostat for your church?

> "'If you can'?" said Jesus. "Everything is possible for him who believes."
> (*Mark 9 v23, NIV*)

What has set the thermostat for your church?

> 'If you have faith and do not doubt... you can say to this mountain, 'Go, throw yourself into the sea,' and it will be done. If you believe, you will receive whatever you ask for in prayer."
> (*Matthew 21 v 21, NIV*)

What has set the thermostat for your church?

> "I tell you the truth, anyone who has faith in me will do what I have been doing. He will do even greater things than these, because I am going to the Father."
>
> (*John 14 v12, NIV*)

So what did Jesus do that we can do even greater things? He healed people from all sorts of illnesses (like deafness, blindness, bleeding, leprosy and fevers.) He cured the paralysed, carried out exorcisms, had dominion over nature and raised the dead. He saw people's futures and pasts, He set people free from shame and guilt, He walked on water and fed people supernaturally.

So with all of that in mind, and with John 14 v12 ringing in our ears, my question is "What do I consider too much for God?"

So what has set the thermostat for your church?

We need to step out into all that is possible and believe that God will supply every need we have.

> *"But I have received everything in full and have an abundance; I am amply supplied... And my God will supply all your needs according to His riches in glory in Christ Jesus."*
>
> (*Philippians 4 v18, NASB*)

WHAT HAS SET THE THERMOSTAT FOR YOUR CHURCH?

Trying and not happening?

So what happens when you try for what's possible and it doesn't happen?

Often, the only time we learn is when we encounter pain. Because it's easier not to change, we keep doing what we're doing until we hit a brick wall.

Take our health, for example. When do we change diets and start exercising? It's when our body is falling apart and the doctor tells us if we don't change our lifestyle, we'll die. All of a sudden - we're motivated!

And in relationships - when do we tell each other how much we care? Usually, when the relationship is failing.

More people than I can remember tell me that they only start praying when the problem has already occurred and everything has gone wrong!

We learn our biggest lessons when things get rough. When we're on our knees after disasters, knock-backs and mistakes - it's then that we say to ourselves, "I'm sick of being broke! Sick of being kicked around! I'm tired of being mediocre! I'm going to do something!"

We celebrate success, but don't learn much from it.

Failure hurts, but that's when we get educated.

Effective people don't go looking for problems, but when they find pain, they ask themselves, "how do I need to change what I'm thinking and what I'm doing, so I can avoid this pain in the future?"

Too many people ignore all the warning signs but when the roof falls in they ask, "why does everything happen to me?" We are creatures of habit - we keep doing what we are doing until we are forced to change.

Think of Israel. God was always nudging them gently and giving them signals, but when they ignored the signals, God decides to nudge them with a sledgehammer: look at the plagues on Egypt, they get more and more serious and more and more painful. Proverbs says *"Listen to my instruction and be wise; do not ignore it."***(Proverbs 8 v33, NIV)** Growth is most painful when we resist it.

Let me show you this principle from Luke:

"A man planted a vineyard, rented it to some farmers and went away for a long time. At harvest time he sent a servant to the tenants so they would give him some of the fruit of the vineyard. But the tenants beat him and sent him away empty-handed. He sent another servant, but that one also they beat and treated shamefully and sent away empty-handed. He sent still a third, and they wounded him and threw him out.

"Then the owner of the vineyard said, 'What shall I do? I will send my son, whom I love; perhaps they will respect him.'"But when the tenants saw him, they talked the matter over. 'This is the heir,' they said. 'Let's kill him, and the inheritance will be ours.' So they threw him out of the vineyard and killed him. "What then will the owner of the vineyard do to them? He will come and kill those tenants and give the vineyard to others." When the

> *people heard this, they said, "May this never be!" Jesus looked directly at them and asked, "Then what is the meaning of that which is written: "'The stone the builders rejected has become the capstone'? Everyone who falls on that stone will be broken to pieces, but he on whom it falls will be crushed."*
>
> *(Luke 20 v9-17, NIV)*

The tenants kept on ignoring the message they were receiving until it ultimately led to their death! God's way is that throughout our life He is wanting to give us useful lessons, happening in His perfect order so that we might learn the lesson He wants to teach us in order to help us move on.

When we don't learn the lesson, we get to take them again and again and again.

Missing a lesson

If we are unhappy everyday then it is likely we have missed a lesson. When we keep losing jobs, partners, friends, money - maybe it's a sign that we haven't been paying attention and learning the lesson God knows we need to learn.

Now, before you get offended - let me show you this principle at work in the Bible.

> *"The Lord will make you the head, not the tail. If you pay attention to the commands of the Lord your God that I give you this day and carefully follow them, you will always be at the top, never at the bottom."*
> *(Deuteronomy 28 v13, NIV)*

God is not here to punish us but to teach and support us. Every event has the potential to transform us and disasters have the greatest potential to change our thinking. Act as if every event has a purpose and your life will have purpose, and if you can figure out why you needed to learn that particular lesson you can conquer it!

Think of Joseph, who at any point could have given up, but rather he kept learning the lesson and moving on to the next one, which eventually taught him how to run Egypt, the superpower of the age!

> *"Take the old prophets as your mentors. They put up with anything, went through everything, and never once quit, all the time honouring God. What a gift life is to those*

who stay the course! You've heard, of course, of Job's staying power, and you know how God brought it all together for him at the end. That's because God cares, cares right down to the last detail."
(*James 5 v10, MSG*)

Finally, if at first you don't succeed, follow your mum's advice -

Try
Try
And try
again!

I want to challenge you to believe in what is possible when you give regularly, or tithe. And I want you to expand your thinking so you can receive all God has to offer when you give over and above your regular tithe with an offering.

> *"Honour the Lord with your wealth, with the first fruits of all your crops; then your barns will be filled to overflowing, and your vats will brim over with new wine."*
> (*Proverbs 3 v9-10, NIV*)

The practice of giving ten per cent of all our wealth to God began in Hebrew history, way before the Law was given to Moses. The first recorded instance is in Genesis when Abraham brought his tithe to the priest of God, Melchizedek, and the second recorded instance was when Jacob made a lifelong commitment to tithe (see Genesis 14 v17-20 and 28 v 20-22.)

Tithing was already a principle in action before the Law was given to Moses, and as such it is an **affirmation** of our faith in God and a recognition that it is all His and comes from Him - He is the source, He is the provider. It confirms our expectation of God's provision in our lives and our faith that He will go on providing.

Not only that, you'll find that tithing is a New Testament principle too!

The idea of tithing appears eight times between Matthew and Hebrews, including here:

> *"Woe to you, scribes and Pharisees, hypocrites! For you **tithe** mint and dill and cummin, and have neglected the weightier*

> *provisions of the law: justice and mercy and faithfulness. But these are the things you should have done without neglecting the others."*
>
> (*Matthew 23 v23, NASB*)

Jesus was saying that the Pharisees should tithe as well as do justice and love God. He saw it as totally normal and did not seek to replace the practice but seems to acknowledge that it is one that we should keep on doing.

All the verses in the New Testament endorse tithing, and also talk about offerings as a way to see increase.

Malachi gives us a massive insight into the tithing principle, showing us the need for it has not ceased:

> *"Yet from the days of your fathers you have gone away from My ordinances and have not kept them. Return to Me, and I will return to you," says the Lord of hosts. "But you said, 'In what way shall we return?'*
>
> *"Will a man rob God? Yet you have robbed Me! But you say, 'In what way have we robbed You?' In tithes and offerings. You are cursed with a curse, for you have robbed Me, even this whole nation. Bring all the tithes into the storehouse, that there may be food in My house.*
>
> *"And try Me now in this," says the Lord of hosts, "If I will not open for you the windows of heaven and pour out for you such blessing that there will not be room enough to receive it. And I will rebuke the devourer for your sakes, so that he will not destroy the fruit of*

> your ground, nor shall the vine fail to bear fruit for you in the field," says the Lord of hosts; "And all nations will call you blessed, for you will be a delightful land," says the Lord of hosts.
> *(Malachi 3 v7-12, NKJV)*

God mentions us robbing Him in two ways - in tithes, and in offerings. The consequences of not tithing or not giving an offering is that there is a curse on our finances - so to understand why not tithing is a robbery, we need to read Leviticus:

> *"And all the tithe of the land, whether of the seed of the land or of the fruit of the tree, is the Lord's. It is holy to the Lord."*
> *(Leviticus 27 v30, NIV)*

The tithe already belongs to God, it is not ours and He expects us to acknowledge that. So to not tithe, or to not give an offering, is to rob from God and to be brought under a curse - so what is the answer to this?

GIVE.
And give **FREELY**.
And **CHEERFULLY**.

So, what happens when we tithe?

1. There is food or supply in God's house. Malachi is explicit that by tithing there will be supply or food in His house, and Hebrews 3 v6 and 1 Peter 2 v5 both talk about God's house as the church. So God is saying there will be food or supplies in HIS house: so the tithe is for the local church that you attend.

2. The rest of Malachi is about the windows of heaven which are opened over your life when you tithe. Remember, when you tithe, you are not **giving** to God, you are **returning** what God has given to you. You are proving faithful, which is important because it establishes a position of trust. It has opened up the window of God's abundant supply to you. This reinforces the principle that as you are giving to God, He will make sure you receive from Him.

3. Finally, God **reverses** the curse and will protect your finances.

Now, with the windows of heaven open and blessings of abundance flowing down to us, it is down to our offerings to establish the measure that God will use to pour blessings down on us.

So, if you tithe ten per cent and return to God what is His, you are living under open windows that your tithe has opened up. God's word is give and it will be given unto you (Luke 6 v38) but we know we can't give God the tithe because He already owns that - what we can give to God is our offering. The measure we use is the measure that God will use - God is ready to give you the blessing, He just wants to know what size scoop to use. God will ensure you receive in the same measure you give.

The tithe opens up the windows of heaven and the offering determines the measure of the blessing you get back.

Or, as 2 Corinthians 9 v6 puts it,

> "He who sows sparingly will also reap sparingly, and he who sows bountifully will also reap bountifully."

I challenge you: become a good steward of what God has given you and start tithing today.

Watch as you live under an open heaven, free from fear.

Then watch what is given back to you as you give your offerings above and beyond your tithe.

As you become a good steward and be rich in good deeds, God starts to notice and gets more to you!

> "Whoever can be trusted with very little can also be trusted with much, and whoever is dishonest with very little will also be dishonest with much. So if you have not been trustworthy in handling worldly wealth, who will trust you with true riches? And if you have not been trustworthy with someone else's property, who will give you property of your own?"
> (*Luke 16 v10, NIV*)

Which leads us to the final challenge Paul makes to the rich: *"Command them to do good, to be rich in deeds, and to be generous and willing to share."* (*1 Timothy 6 v18, NIV*) Once they are liberated from the magnet of pride (the delusion that 'I am in control, I am responsible for my success') and once their hope is set on God, not money, only one thing can happen: their money will flow freely to make happen what is in God's heart.

Imagine abundant churches who give and give and yet

keep receiving, who continually give to the poor, the lonely, the lost, to new businesses, to communities and to newly married couples who need help to buy a home.

How amazing would it be if we were lending the world money? How great would it be if there was a cure for AIDS, but it was too expensive, so the church paid for it for the world?

This is why God wants to give us so much!

In Ephesians, Paul says, *"He who has been stealing must steal no longer, but must work, doing something useful with his own hands, that he may have something to share with those in need." (Ephesians 4 v28, NIV)* In other words, there are three levels of how to live with things:

1. you can steal to get;
2. you can work to get;
3. you can work to get in order to give.

Too many professing Christians live on level two. Almost all the forces of our culture *urge* them to live on level two. But the Bible pushes us passionately to level three:

"God is able to make all grace abound to you, so that always having all sufficiency in everything, you may have an abundance for every good deed."
(*2 Corinthians 9 v8, NASB*)

Why does God bless us with abundance? So that we can have more than enough to live on (like the birds who have an abundance of worms and trees) and then use the rest for all sorts of good works that remove spiritual and physical misery. There is more than enough for us and there is an abundance for others.

The issue is not how much a person makes. Big industry and big salaries are a fact of life, and they are not evil. The evil is in not being a good steward of what God has given you.

Perhaps even the evil is in a poverty mentality that we have been shackled into believing is God's plan for us.

Some Money Tips...

As we said at the beginning, the point here is purpose – do we pursue a luxuriant lifestyle, or give all our money away? But that's missing the point of everything that Jesus taught about money. He called us to lose our lives in order that we might gain them again (and the context is indeed money, "What does it profit a man, to gain the whole world and forfeit his soul?" *Mark 8 v36, NASB.*) And the way He means for us to lose our lives is in fulfilling the mission of love He gave us. The point is purpose – what is it, and how does it drive us – and with that context, abundance can begin!

There is a new day dawning in the church as we wake up to all that God has for us and wants to get done through us. Remember, the local church is the hope of the world.

Believe that there is thousands of pounds locked up in everyone, and millions of pounds locked up in every church.

God is looking for men and women who will finance His local church - He is looking for you to break through.

Decide to have a prosperous mindset and commit yourself to putting in the necessary effort

Give to God first then save and spend what is left

EIGHT TIPS TO

Observe wealthy people and model their successful behaviours – ask questions if possible

Humble yourself and ask for some help from those further on in their journey than you

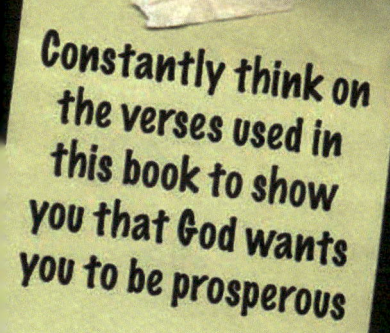

Constantly think on the verses used in this book to show you that God wants you to be prosperous

Make plans and set goals

DEVELOP ABUNDANCE

Spoil yourself occasionally - to remind yourself you are very precious in God's sight

Continually stretch your belief system as to what is possible for you to achieve

Choose not to take OFFENCE

For some of you, the message in this book may have been offensive, but that was not my intention. Some of you may may have found it provocative, which definitely was my intention, to stir us up to love and good deeds and get us talking about the reality of the situation, to recognise that something must be done right now before we sleepwalk into oblivion, waffling on about how everything is fine.

I believe in the local church because Jesus believes in the local church. I believe it is the hope of the world and I know it can do and be all that God wants it to be! Yet unless we first acknowledge how bad the situation really is we won't take the drastic action that is necessary so the church will still exist fifty years from now. Once we have realised how dire the situation is then maybe some of us will take the drastic action that is necessary and stop settling for anything less than the best. Perhaps then leaders will begin to lead.

I am convinced that once we are fully aware of the situation we can turn the situation around by putting into practice the five main steps I have outlined:

1. Getting a new map
2. Leadership
3. Knowing your outcomes and your goals
4. Attracting the next generation
5. Gaining an abundance mindset

To help some of you, I believe that God has called us to a journey, not a destiny. In Matthew 4 v19, Jesus called the disciples to follow Him, a journey that would transform their lives.

So let me ask you a question, when was the last time you let something change or transform you?

Could this book help challenge, cajole and push you into making some necessary changes to help the local church continue to be the hope of the world?

I hope so. God hopes so.

And the only person stopping you from this bright new dawn... is you!

Bible Notes
NASB – New American Standard Bible
NIV – New International Version
NKJV – New King James Version
NLT – New Living Translation
MSG – The Message

Image Notes
All images are used with permission.
Image p6, © Global York
Image p8, 15 © 2474254, istockphoto.com
Scream p. 11, © 2505657, istockphoto.com
Business Prophet p. 16, © 3040444, istockphoto.com
Gold silver bullet on black p.24, © 3106779, istockphoto.com
Denial p. 25, © 2694919, istockphoto.com
apocalypse p. 44, © 3109338, istockphoto.com
Image p53, © 2631584, istockphoto.com
King of matches p. 58, © 2761788, istockphoto.com
Business Vision p. 61, © 2064985, istockphoto.com
Airport Sign p. 68, © 2709595, istockphoto.com
City Rockers p. 74, © 3165353, istockphoto.com
Strategy p. 75, © 2767460, istockphoto.com
bungee jump p. 80, © 1935273, istockphoto.com
Money Rain p. 90, © 3581916, istockphoto.com
Retro air controls p. 104, © 435028, istockphoto.com
Reminder p. 120,121, © 2146002, istockphoto.com
Sea of Clouds p. 122, © 3062553, istockphoto.com

A note on the type
Wake Up Dead Man is published in Bau.